STUDIES IN ECONOMIC AND SOCIAL HISTORY

This series, specially commissioned by the Economic History Society, provides a guide to the current interpretations of the key themes of economic and social history in which advances have recently been made or in which there has been significant debate.

Originally entitled 'Studies in Economic History', in 1974 the series had its scope extended to include topics in social history, and the new series title, 'Studies in Economic and Social History', signalises this development.

The series gives readers access to the best work done, helps them to draw their own conclusions in major fields of study, and by means of the critical bibliography in each book guides them in the selection of further reading. The aim is to provide a springboard to further work rather than a set of pre-packaged conclusions or short-cuts.

ECONOMIC HISTORY SOCIETY

The Economic History Society, which numbers over 3000 members, publishes the *Economic History Review* four times a year (free to members) and holds an annual conference. Enquiries about membership should be addressed to the Assistant Secretary, Economic History Society, Peterhouse, Cambridge. Full-time students may join at special rates.

D0924111

STUDIES IN ECONOMIC AND SOCIAL HISTORY

Edited for the Economic History Society by T. C. Smout

PUBLISHED

OTHER TITLES ARE IN PREPARATION

Economic Foundations of British Overseas Expansion 1815–1914

Prepared for
The Economic History Society

P. J. CAIN
Senior Lecturer in Economic History
University of Birmingham

© The Economic History Society 1980

All rights reserved. No part of this publication
may be reproduced or transmitted, in any form
or by any means, without permission.

First published 1980 by
THE MACMILLAN PRESS LTD
London and Basingstoke
Associated companies in Delhi Dublin
Hong Kong Johannesburg Lagos Melbourne
New York Singapore and Tokyo

Printed in Hong Kong

British Library Cataloguing in Publication Data

Cain, P J
    Economic foundations of British overseas
    expansion, 1815–1914. – (Studies in economic
    and social history).
    1. Great Britain – Economic conditions – 19th
    century   2. Great Britain – Economic conditions
    – 20th century
    3. Great Britain – Economic policy
    I. Title   II. Series
    330.9′41′07   HC255

    ISBN 0–333–23284–4

This book is sold subject to the standard
conditions of the Net Book Agreement.

The paperback edition of this book is sold subject to the condition that it shall
not, by way of trade or otherwise, be lent, resold, hired out, or otherwise
circulated without the publisher's prior consent in any form of binding or cover
other than that in which it is published and without a similar condition
including this condition being imposed on the subsequent purchaser.

Contents

Note on References

References in the text within square brackets relate to the numbered items in the Select Bibliography, followed, where necessary, by the page numbers in italics, for example [153: *10*].

Editor's Preface

SINCE 1968, when the Economic History Society and Macmillan published the first of the 'Studies in Economic and Social History', the series has established itself as a major teaching tool in universities, colleges and schools, and as a familiar landmark in serious bookshops throughout the country. A great deal of the credit for this must go to the wise leadership of its first editor, Professor M. W. Flinn, who retired at the end of 1977. The books tend to be bigger now than they were originally, and inevitably more expensive; but they have continued to provide information in modest compass at a reasonable price by the standards of modern academic publications.

There is no intention of departing from the principles of the first decade. Each book aims to survey findings and discussion in an important field of economic or social history that has been the subject of recent lively debate. It is meant as an introduction for readers who are not themselves professional researchers but who want to know what the discussion is all about – students, teachers and others generally interested in the subject. The authors, rather than either taking a strongly partisan line or suppressing their own critical faculties, set out the arguments and the problems as fairly as they can, and attempt a critical summary and explanation of them from their own judgement. The discipline now embraces so wide a field in the study of the human past that it would be inappropriate for each book to follow an identical plan, but all volumes will normally contain an extensive descriptive bibliography.

The series is not meant to provide all the answers but to help readers to see the problems clearly enough to form their own conclusions. We shall never agree in history, but the discipline will be well served if we know what we are disagreeing about, and why.

University of Edinburgh

T. C. SMOUT
Editor

Introduction

THIS pamphlet differs from previous ones in two ways. First, it examines a rather broader theme than previous works in this series. Secondly, it provides a link between previous pamphlets on various aspects of the development of the traditional leading industrial nations and new pamphlets in this series dealing with other parts of the world. Two of these pamphlets on the new theme – by Dr N. Charlesworth on India and by Dr I. McPherson on Japan – are already in preparation. I should also emphasise that although the pamphlet is based on the assumption that economic forces played an important role in imperial expansion throughout the century, this is not meant to imply that political, religious or other non-economic motives were of no importance. In this survey they are, if only for reasons of space, simply omitted from consideration.

The writing of this pamphlet has been made a great deal easier because of the expert help I have been able to rely on from my colleagues in the Economic and Social History Department in Birmingham. Both Professor A. G. Hopkins and Dr I. G. Brown have given me a great deal of excellent advice and criticism and I am heavily indebted to them. I should also like to thank Professor J. R. Harris, Professor T. C. Smout and Dr G. Studdert-Kennedy for their interest and encouragement. None of these are of course responsible for my errors or omissions. Mrs Yvonne Jacobs and Miss Shirley Swann deserve medals for the skilful and speedy way in which they translated my execrable handwriting into type.

Finally, I should like to dedicate this little book to my wife Christine, who encouraged and sustained me whilst I was writing it, and to my children, Ruth and Eleanor.

Part I *1815-75*

1 Theoretical Approaches

IN 1815, British economic foreign policy was still largely dominated by ideas which had been inherited from the nation's pre-industrial past and which, following Adam Smith, historians and economists have labelled 'mercantilist'. Given the relatively slow growth of agriculture in the early modern period, the mercantilists looked to trade as one of the few means of increasing wealth and power rapidly. Agricultural produce was difficult to export and emphasis was placed on the need for the export of manufactures, the control of luxury trades and dominance of the carrying trade. International commerce was slow to expand and this explains the interest of nations in trade diversion and in colonial possessions with their obvious implications for international conflict.

Control over foreign trade was also ensured by a host of protective devices. In 1815, Britain was still a protectionist power and the state played an important role in directing foreign trade and overseas expansion. Tariff protection was extended not only to agriculture but also to Britain's growing manufacturing industries. Severe restrictions were placed upon the emigration of skilled labour and the export of machinery in an attempt to prevent foreign nations from acquiring the power to emulate Britain's growing supremacy in industry and technology. The Navigation Acts tried to ensure that as much trade as possible was carried in British ships manned by British crews. In this case the objective was partly to direct the profits of shipping into British hands, partly to ensure that, in the absence of a large professional navy, men and ships would always be available for defence. The East India Company, with monopoly trading rights in its appointed subcontinent, was thought to have better prospects of increasing the wealth of the nation through foreign trade than were individual traders. And most informed statesmen still felt it important to maintain a colonial empire. Colonies provided both secure markets and sources of supply – which could be fostered by giving the colonies preferences in British markets – and were the most fertile ground within which the Navigation Laws could flourish.

By 1815, however, this state-directed autarchic policy with its obvious warlike and imperialist assumptions was being called into question. At the end of the Napoleonic Wars, Britain had clearly become the world's most advanced industrial nation and, in these circumstances, it could be argued that protectionism was no longer necessary. Discarding the idea that international trade was static and that one nation's gain was another's loss, some thinkers went on to argue for a system of free trade in the world which would promote international division of labour and specialisation and bring economic benefits to all the participants. Out of this free trade radical approach grew the belief that the spread of international trade on capitalist principles would bring not only universal wealth but also an end to international conflict; growth and mutual benefit could now be attained by interdependence rather than by trade wars and colonialism. In this schema, war and overseas expansion were believed to be the product of feudalism, expressing the warlike propensities of the landed aristocracy and the needs of the commercial and financial classes directly dependent on them who had often used the state to create vested interests and monopolies. The waste of resources in war and imperialism had inhibited growth in the past; but the development of capitalism was confidently expected to eliminate these archaic forces eventually. The clearest academic presentation of the argument that capitalism was an essentially peaceful and anti-imperialist mode of production, and that the continuation of imperialism and colonialism into the capitalist era was to be put down to the survival of pre-capitalist elements which would eventually disappear, is in the work of Schumpeter [165]. The idea was, however, something of a commonplace with generations of middle-class radicals from the time of Smith onwards [9: esp. 32–59; 105: esp. 29–34; 17].

Free trade and a hostility to overseas domination did not necessarily go together in the nineteenth century. There was a line of argument, originating with Josiah Tucker in the mid-eighteenth century, which, while clearly recognising that Britain's increasing competitive strength made free trade a sensible policy, yet gave free trade a mercantilist twist. From this viewpoint, it was useful for Britain to abandon protection and to persuade others to do the same because, given Britain's growing technological lead, free trade would ensure that Britain's rivals did not develop in the same way and would remain dependent primary producers. Britain could, therefore, abandon colonialism and protection and yet retain through 'free trade imperialism', economic and political hegemony as the chief centre of industrial wealth [170: 14–24; 169].

This controversy between the radical anti-imperialists and the free trade imperialists in the eighteenth and nineteenth centuries has, to some degree, been reproduced in the modern controversy between Gallagher and Robinson and Platt.

Writing in 1953, when an anti-imperialist view of the early nineteenth century was prevalent, Gallagher and Robinson attacked the assumption that it was sufficient, when discussing British imperialism, to concern oneself solely with the places painted a British red on the map and with extensions of what they called 'formal' control. They shifted attention to that large area of the globe which, without being subject to British sovereignty, was none the less controlled or strongly influenced by British economic and political power. The previous obsession with formal empire as opposed to the 'informal' one of economic, political and cultural influence was, they argued, 'rather like judging the size and character of icebergs solely from the point above the waterline' [57: 1].

After 1815, Britain's main interest overseas was, according to Gallagher and Robinson, in extending her informal control sufficiently to integrate as many areas as possible into her expanding economy with its need for constantly widening markets and new sources of supply. This desire to 'limit the use of paramount power to establishing security for trade' is contrasted with the eighteenth-century policy of 'commercial imperialism and monopoly through political possession' [57: 6]. The transference from one to the other reflected the growing confidence of Britain in her ability to dominate world markets through free trade and the businessman's natural aversion from the taxes, interfering governments and bureaucracy which inevitably accompanied formal annexation and control.

The simple notion of a 'free trade imperialism' was then qualified somewhat. It was admitted that control was often extended beyond the area of economic development itself to others which were vital for their strategic protection. Furthermore, it had to be recognised that, however closely tied they were to Britain economically, the other great powers could not be controlled informally; and their influence could sometimes prevent or mitigate British control of smaller, weaker areas which would otherwise have felt Britain's power more strongly. None the less, in those places where the British had a free hand politically they were not averse, Gallagher and Robinson claim, from interfering in the internal affairs of smaller, weaker states to ensure the right conditions for the maintenance of their commercial hegemony. This process was greatly facilitated by the fact that, as the greatest naval power, the

British were the neighbours of everyone with a coastline. In cases where informal means of control proved inappropriate, the British were not slow to abandon them for formal control. State power was applied in India both to control her politically and to tie her closely to the British economy; and an impressive number of places were translated from the sphere of informality into dominions of the Crown even before 1870. In Gallagher and Robinson's words, Britain's policy might be summarised as 'trade with informal control if possible, trade with rule when necessary' [57: 6].

In a later article, Robinson has made it clearer than before that, in his view, the parts of the world most dominated by Britain were often those which had political independence, such as the Latin American countries or the white colonies after 1850. They were peopled by 'ideal prefabricated collaborators' who almost instinctively geared the economic life of their new settlements to fit in with the needs of Britain [159: 124-6]. In so doing they are said to be prime examples of what Richard Graham has called 'cultural imperialism' where countries are so affected by the success of Britain that they uncritically accept her economic ideology and become her economic appendages [67]. Countries with a different cultural tradition could not be dominated in this way and this is why, in order to be integrated into the world economy, India and China had either to be formally controlled or occasionally bullied into compliance with British aims.

Platt, in his attacks on Gallagher and Robinson's position, has reaffirmed, though from a different perspective, the view that Britain was disinclined towards imperial expansion in the early part of the nineteenth century. He believes Gallagher and Robinson have over-estimated the extent to which British governments were intent on interference in the affairs of others for commercial purposes. Platt claims that the main concern of government was in negotiating Open Door or most-favoured nation treaties which would prevent discrimination against British products, persons and property. This 'opening up' of markets did sometimes lead to violence as in China: but the British usually limited themselves to rectifying treaty violations and protecting lives and property. Bondholders who relied on the navy to force debtors to pay defaulted loans were usually told they should have invested their funds at home; and the Foreign Office was wary of using its influence, if only because of fears that this might give some individuals a competitive advantage over others when the governmental role was to ensure equality of treatment for all. Traders abroad were also hostile to government interference which could wreck carefully cultivated relationships with local élites or mean formal control and taxation [149].

In later writings, Platt has gone further and argued that the lack of interest in 'informal' empire was a reflection of the lack of any real stimulus to economic expansion overseas. Britain was agriculturally self-sufficient until late in the nineteenth century and, between 1800 and 1850, the emphasis was on the growth of domestic investment and the home market. The relatively small demand for foreign supplies and outlets could be met quite adequately through either traditional markets in Europe or America, or the existing empire. Not only was the growth of exports slow but the steady determination, up until the 1840s, to maintain protection and imperial preference meant that the possibilities of trade with new areas outside the system was restricted. In fact, Platt argues that the maintenance of a protectionist and colonial system is a clear indication of the basic lack of interest in markets in the so-called informal empire. Besides which, he claims that these newer markets in Latin America, the Ottoman Empire and the Far East were not only unnecessary but largely inaccessible before the coming of the railway. Except during moments of speculative optimism, British businessmen and traders were, according to Platt, well aware of this. There was, in short, neither the need for nor the ability to acquire an informal economic empire after 1815 [152; 153]. If the boundaries of empire continued to expand this was not because British governments felt it necessary but because of problems on the periphery 'which cannot exclude the economic ambitions of the frontiersman on the move into empty territory ahead' [153: 10]. Platt here accepts a Galbraithian explanation of frontier movement: the expansion of the imperial boundary was often caused by 'turbulence' on the frontier which lead the 'men-on-the-spot' to take action which the metropolitan government had to accept [47].

A very different perspective can be attained by looking at the relationship between fluctuations and crises in the British economy and attitudes to overseas expansion in this period. E. G. Wakefield, writing in the 1830s, portrayed an economy with a tendency towards an oversupply of capital, leading to distress and unemployment. This he put down to severe restrictions on the 'field of employment' of British capital, by which he meant the lack of effective demand arising from the agricultural sector. To offset this, Wakefield wanted free trade to enhance the international division of labour and encourage the better exploitation of Britain's colonial possessions, making them into Britain's granaries which could siphon off not only manufactured exports but

15

also surplus capital and labour [168]. Marx, in similar style, posited a falling rate of profit, a tendency to overproduction and to recurrent cyclical crises, and argued that one of the many offsets to these crises and instability was an expanding foreign trade and the export of capital [4: 40–7]. Marx never drew out the imperialist implications of this in any general way, but he did assume a relationship between crises in the British economy and the penetration of Indian and Chinese markets [2].

Nineteenth-century radicals, like Schumpeter, saw a protectionist imperialism dissolving as international capitalism, with its free trade implications, grew in strength. Gallagher and Robinson ignore the protectionist side of policy after 1815 and assume a steady economic expansion of Britain overseas controlled by a policy of 'free trade imperialism' and informal empire. Platt returns to the emphasis on the mercantilist influence on policy after 1815 and denies the need for further expansion, thus reasserting, though for somewhat different reasons, the earlier emphasis on the lack of imperialist impulses emanating from British capitalism after 1815. On the other hand, some contemporary writers, such as Wakefield and Marx, saw a connection between social and economic crises, the need for foreign markets to grow faster, and extensions of formal and informal imperialism. Which, if any, of these general views is nearest the mark will be the subject of the following chapters.

2 The Coming of Free Trade and 'Free Trade Imperialism' after 1815

ONE very pertinent criticism of Gallagher and Robinson is that they assume too readily the existence of a free trade policy in Britain as early as 1815. In fact, free trade won a very slow victory in Britain and was not generally accepted before the 1840s. In 1815, then, there is much to be said for Platt's picture of a self-sufficient Britain meeting her trading needs mainly through contacts with her existing empire and traditional trading partners in the USA and Europe. Platt, however, does not appreciate the extent to which this traditional system began to break down in the aftermath of the Napoleonic Wars.

In the first place, the clamour against restrictions on trade grew as Britain's relative superiority as an industrial producer and exporter became more obvious. Economists such as Smith were arguing at the time of the American Revolution that a system of universal free trade would be to Britain's advantage, and that colonies and protection-ism were unnecessary to commercial success. Progress towards a general acceptance of this view was slow. Pitt's and Shelburne's attempts to apply Smith's reasoning in the 1780s failed, in part because business interests in Britain still feared the competitiveness of overseas rivals [170: *30–44*]. During the Napoleonic Wars, however, the manufacturing sector, led by the cotton interests, began to feel greater confidence in its ability to compete in the domestic market and abroad.

Secondly, the assumption that Britain could remain largely self-sufficient began to be questioned as early as the 1820s. In 1815, a Corn Law was passed in Parliament which disallowed imports until domestic prices reached 80s. a bushel and was clearly designed to ensure the profitability of the extra land brought into cultivation during the Wars. By the early 1820s, the rapidity of population growth and the growing employment problem was already prompting the idea that Britain should try to encourage agricultural imports in return for her own manufactured exports. In this way, the increased population would in the long term be sure of manufacturing employment and cheap and abundant food. Within a very few years, pressure was already building up to modify the Corn Law of 1815 in such a way as to encourage potential agricultural suppliers, especially those in Europe [79: esp. *78f.*, *294f.*].

Thirdly, after 1815, loss or disruption of existing markets increased the pressure to move to freer trade. The successful attack on the East India Company's trading monopoly in India in 1813, owed some of its strength to the rising optimism of private enterprise; but it was also a response to the restrictions placed upon exports at that time by the Napoleonic and American Wars, [195: *445*; 138]. Similarly, the merchant's petition of 1820, asking for freer trade and complaining about the costs of agricultural protection, came out of a mixture of increasing business self-assertiveness and anxieties about overseas sales when post-war European markets were depressed [195: *446-9*; 170: *135*].

The growing feeling for Britain's competitive strength and the need for more export markets and secure food supplies, lay behind the Tory government's moves towards freer trade in the 1820s. Some duties on manufactured imports were abolished; the 1815 Corn Law was replaced by a milder variant, based on a sliding scale, in 1828; tariff levels were adjusted downwards generally; the Navigation Acts were trimmed and shipping agreements entered into with foreign countries on the basis of reciprocity [79]. The reforms were very limited in effect. Protection was still accepted as necessary to 'equalize the disadvantages of the British manufacturer burdened by higher wages and taxes than his rivals' [195: *445*] and the changes in the shipping laws did not infringe the British monopoly of colonial traffic. Liberal reforms had to make their way very slowly, impeded by vociferous opposition from both industrial and landed interests in Britain and the colonies [12: chs 10 and 11]. In 1830 the free trade movement had only just begun but the view that Britain's future growth and prosperity depended more upon industry and trade than upon land was making progress rapidly in political circles [79: *305-6*].

In the 1830s and early 1840s, as population increase, industrial crisis and instability prompted movements of social and political protest such as Chartism, the pressure for freer trade became more intense. The mounting hostility to the Corn Laws was based on the probably erroneous assumption that they raised food prices and also reduced output by pushing up manufacturers' costs. Some businessmen saw the repeal of the Corn Laws as a pretext for cutting wages, but the obvious general unpopularity of this argument led many of the Anti-Corn Law League's leaders to reformulate their position. Emphasis in the 1840s was placed upon the need to encourage agricultural and raw-material imports so that foreigners could more easily earn the sterling they needed to buy British exports and thus boost output and employment [68: ch 5; 36].

By the 1830s too, worries about competition from tariff-protected European and American industry were becoming acute. Businessmen could hope that the freer trade became, the greater would be the possibility of crushing the incipient industrialism of others. The attempts made in the 1830s to induce European countries to make concessions on the basis of reciprocity were often founded on the notion that there ought to be a 'natural' division of labour between industrial Britain and agricultural Europe. These negotiations failed largely because countries like France were determined to avoid dependence on Britain for their manufactured commodities. Many free trade interests failed to appreciate this and argued that a unilateral movement towards free trade by Britain was necessary and would, eventually, induce free trade elsewhere [12: *108–10, 121–3, 132–3, 195–6*].

The movement towards tariff reform in the 1840s can be seen as the recognition by the political élite that free trade might help to solve the socio-economic crisis by encouraging more rapid industrial growth. Peel's free trade budgets of 1842 and 1845, and the further modification and then repeal of the Corn Laws in 1842 and 1846 [166: *145–65*], were the outcome of this changed perspective on Britain's future. Peel hoped to establish Britain firmly as the world's foremost industrial power by opening her market to agricultural supplies from as wide an area as possible. Reinforced by cheap imports, Britain could stay permanently ahead of her industrial rivals and, hopefully, underline her economic hegemony by persuading them to adopt free trade themselves [170: *146–50*].

This 'free trade imperialist' strain in British thinking has tended to be underrated, partly because Richard Cobden, the most prominent member of the Anti-Corn Law League in the 1840s, was himself very idealistic about free trade and its effects. Like Adam Smith and James Mill, Cobden assumed that free trade would produce an international division of labour which would be equally beneficial to all the participants, industrialists and primary producers alike. He looked forward to a world of interdependent nations amongst whom wealth and power would be widely diffused and whose self-interest would lead them to abolish warfare and sweep aside the aristocratic class and their dependents who benefited from the old system of restriction, monopoly and imperialism [17; 115; 170: *159–63*].

Average opinion amongst businessmen in Manchester and elsewhere was different from this. They were obsessed with the need to retain Britain's commercial supremacy. Free trade was seen as a weapon in this commercial war, and when it did not seem to answer to their needs it was not supported. For example, despite their vigorous support for free trade in corn, business interests for long retained their belief in the need to prevent the export of skilled labour or machinery for fear that this would encourage competition abroad. The prohibition on artisan emigration was, in fact, dropped as early as 1824 but more because it had proved impossible to enforce than for any other reason. The iron masters strongly supported prohibition in 1824 and textile manufacturers were divided on the issue. Machinery was officially allowed out of Britain under licence after 1825 and the textile interests did their best to restrict export to obsolete models or to those which did not obviously set up direct competition with British manufacturers. This proved equally impossible to enforce. Besides this, Manchester's stance on machinery exports proved embarrassing politically in view of their campaign against the Corn Laws: and the machine-building section of the textile trades had grown, by the 1840s, to the point where export markets were necessary to maintain prosperity. The restriction on exports was lifted, but only in 1843. Manchester had decided that, if it was impossible to kill off the industry of others by restrictions on the export of capital and labour, then perhaps Corn Law repeal might do the trick instead [90; 139].

The pragmatism which inspired the free trade movement can also be appreciated by looking at the abolition of the Navigation Acts in 1849 and 1850. This was not accomplished without considerable misgivings. The ability of British carriers to compete against all-comers was questionable and there were worries about naval defence. Pressure to abolish the Acts grew only slowly after Huskisson's initial reforms of the 1820s. The steady growth of a professional navy made the defence argument less relevant; and, once the white colonies were denied their preferences in the British market, as was the case from the 1840s, it was difficult to expect them to abide by such restrictions. None the less many voices were raised in the debates upon abolition about the possible loss of trade and the implications for national security. The protests were in vain: the Acts were abolished and with them the last great bulwark of the 'old colonial policy' [23].

Between 1815 and the 1850s Britain emerged from a state-directed protectionist policy to one of free trade. But the latter was not so much the product of an optimistic consciousness of industrial superiority as a pragmatic reaction to the crises in the internal economy and growing difficulty in finding secure markets overseas. The policy of free trade, as it emerged in the 1840s, also had strong imperialist overtones.

3   British Economic Policy and the Empire

(i) THE WHITE SETTLED COLONIES

IN 1815, the white settled colonies were still very much a part of an economic and political system ruled firmly from Britain and it was a commonplace as late as the 1830s to associate them with commercial and navigational success [171: *82–95*]. The relationship between economic subservience and political control could be seen most obviously when, in 1835 and again in 1842, the white colonies were reminded that legislation passed by their own parliaments would not be approved in Britain if they ceased to give preferential treatment to British goods [195: *453*].

In the first half of the century, a continuous interest was shown in trying to stimulate the growth of colonies and settlements in North America, Australasia and Africa by diverting emigrants to them and away from their chief destination, the USA, whose growth in wealth and power was a source of anxiety to British statesmen. After the Napoleonic Wars, schemes were promoted which made a modest attempt to divert some of the flow to Canada and the Cape. Most of these early efforts were badly conceived failures [91: chs 2 and 3], but emigration policies took on a new dimension when Robert Wilmot Horton became parliamentary under-secretary at the Colonial Office in 1821. Horton believed that the post-war economic crisis in Britain resulted from an excess of labour in relation to the capital available to employ it. The excess could best be dealt with by promoting emigration to the colonies. Horton suggested that the government should lend local authorities money which the latter could use to provide funds for pauper emigrants who would be provided with land in the colonies. The result would be a relief from the burden of the poor rate in Britain and a build up of the colonies, which would increase Britain's security and make them into more valuable economic partners. The initial loans would eventually be paid back partly by the parish and partly by the settlers out of the product of their lands. The mercantilist element in these proposals was marked. Government was to be the directing agency and public spending the key to success. Emigration was seen as a means of social control in Britain and of expanding and consolidating an empire still managed from the centre [91: 60–8; 60; 13].

Several small schemes were promoted along these lines but none was very successful in diverting emigrant flows away from the USA. Interest began to shift to more liberal schemes of emigration, reflecting the slow drift of opinion away from state interference. By 1830, Wakefield was claiming that he could solve the underconsumptionist crisis in Britain by a better use of land in the colonies. Private companies were to be given charters by Parliament which would allow them to sell land in the colonies at a price which only those of middling economic status could afford. The fund thus created would then be used to bring labourers to the colonies who would do wage work for the landholders. This would solve the underconsumptionist crisis in Britain by extending the 'field of employment' for capital, creating a new market for its goods and providing secure, cheap supplies in return [196; 168; 170: chs 4 and 5; 98; 143].

Wakefield's ideas – which received support both in parliament and amongst influential intellectuals such as J. S. Mill – had a much stronger relationship to liberal capitalist notions than did Horton's [91 ch. 10]. But, even though Wakefield preferred to use private companies rather than the state as his moving agency, his scheme still remains a deliberate attempt to utilise colonial territories to increase Britain's wealth and power. Robert Torrens, the influential economist and politician, went even further than Wakefield in arguing in the 1830s and 1840s that there was a vital relationship between colonial economic development and the maintenance of British economic hegemony. Torrens, who was extremely fearful of the growing competitiveness of European industry wanted to buttress Wakefieldism by bringing the colonies into a Zollverein with a common tariff against foreign manufactures and free trade between all parts of the empire [170: 192–8]. There were many other plans put forward for closer political and economic ties between colonies and mother country between 1820 and 1870 which, like Torrens's, might have involved the continued subordination of the younger communities to Britain [127].

Wakefield himself appreciated that the economic development of the colonies on the lines he suggested could not take place without the grant of some degree of local political autonomy. His proposals were, however, like those of his friend Lord Durham in the famous report of 1840 on colonial government, carefully hedged about. Control of land policy, tariffs and foreign policy would remain in British hands, leaving the colonies with what Wakefield accurately described as 'municipal self-government' [126: 53–9].

Once free trade was established, the policy of Wakefield and Durham was difficult to implement. Radicals, such as Cobden and Bright, argued that the only reason for colonies – exclusive markets – had now disappeared so it was reasonable to give them political as well as economic independence. While they were governed from Britain, useless and expensive wars on their behalf were always a possibility and they would never attain to any economic or political maturity. It would be better to separate from them, relying on the fellow feeling which came from racial kinship and economic interdependence to provide the rationale for future close relations [105: ch. 3; 48; 35: ch. 2].

After 1850 it was recognised that it would be impossible to retain control over the colonies by the means suggested by Durham and Wakefield because the acceptance of free trade and more cosmopolitan attitudes to economic expansion made their deliberate colonialism seem redundant. Free trade also meant the end of colonial privilege and made close political control of colonies, when they had developed maturely, seem impossible to maintain. Statesmen in Britain in the 1840s came to see the colonies as children who were growing up, sometimes very rapidly [105: 76]. Responsible government for colonies began in the late 1840s and gathered pace. Although they retained extensive control in theory, the British quietly let their sovereign powers fall into desuetude. By the 1850s, the Canadian provinces were operating tariffs against Britain, and the Crown's power over land disposal was already in abeyance [126: 59–69]. Self-government was thereafter granted to white-settled territories whenever London felt that they were able to provide stable governments.

The growth of responsible government in the white colonies after 1850 does suggest that the British deliberately abandoned their power and that anti-imperialism was the order of the day [103]. There is much to be said, though, for the view that the British swapped a system of close economic control, which became increasingly inconvenient, for an informal relationship in which economic control was maintained through cultural imperialism [57: 4].

(ii) INDIA

The East India Company's monopoly of Indian trade with Britain was abolished in 1813 when, under pressure of war both in Europe and America, businessmen felt especially anxious about the need to find new markets abroad. Thereafter, Indian import tariffs were fixed at very low levels but with some discrimination in Britain's favour. At the same time, heavy duties were still placed on Indian cloth imports into the British market [78: 7]. By 1840, when competition in European and American markets was keenly felt, pressure to bring India into yet closer economic relations with Britain was growing. The Cotton Supply Association, centred on Manchester and created in 1847, was only the most important group to put pressure on successive British governments to use Indian revenues to build an adequate transport system, and provide other public utilities. This would open up the interior to British textiles and other exports, encourage India as a cotton supplier, and reduce the dependence of Lancashire on the southern states of America, threatened at that time by civil war [175; 78: ch. 3]. As Marx argued, the British had realised that the further penetration of Indian markets could only occur if the dependency was developed sufficiently to supply commodities in payment for British exports [2: *88–95, 132–9*].

The most interesting aspect of these proposals is that Lancashire businessmen, in contradistinction to their usual position on such matters in Britain, worked hard to persuade the East India Company to guarantee a return of 5 per cent on the capital raised for railway projects. They claimed that without guarantees, the capital could not be raised at all. These guarantees were given, partly because the idea of a transport net throughout India was enthusiastically supported by many British politicians and military men in India who saw it as a useful way of extending control. This combined pressure had its effect: steamship services were granted subsidies and many railway schemes were floated in the 1850s under the guarantee system inaugurated in 1849, together with irrigation works, road and river improvement schemes and other public works in which Lancashire, especially, felt it had an interest [187: *1–12, 151f.*; 135; 136: ch. 7]. One consequence of this capital expenditure and the heavy interest payments it involved was that the Indian government needed to borrow in London. After 1850 India rapidly became an important source for the export of British capital [89: ch. 7].

Public-works policies were occasionally reinforced by manipulating the Indian tariff in Lancashire's favour, forcing India into a free-trading relationship with Britain which may have had harmful long-term consequences for the economy. In 1859, faced with the enormous debt created by the Mutiny of 1857 for which Indian rather than British revenues had to provide, the government in India decided to put up tariff rates on imported manufactures, at the same time abolishing the long-standing discrimination against foreigners. The import duty on cotton piece goods was raised from 5 per cent to 10 per cent. In 1859

Lancashire was willing to accept this as a distasteful temporary necessity, but by 1861/2 this acquiescence had disappeared. The effects of the American Civil War on markets and supplies led Manchester men to complain bitterly against the 'unnatural' impositions which they felt were fostering an 'artificial' Indian cotton industry and cutting their sales. Accordingly, the duties on cotton piece goods were reduced to 5 per cent in 1862 [78: 7f.; 77]. The British manufacturing interests did not always get their way. For instance, the financial difficulties of the Indian government brought to a halt the guarantees on railways [175: 112f.; 136: 147, 150], and industrial interests in Britain had always to jostle for position with the military and the bureaucracy in India for power and influence. Also, although the Lancashire lobby continued to influence Indian tariff policy, its power slowly declined in the latter part of the century [101; 76; 188: 342-5].

4   Economic Expansion and Informal Empire after 1815

(i) INFORMAL EMPIRE IN LATIN AMERICA

WE must now examine the relationships between Britain and areas outside the bounds of formal empire. A great deal of the controversy on this issue has centred on Britain's relationships with the Latin American countries so they must be dealt with first. Did the British try to gain economic hegemony through free trade [57: 9–10] or did they simply bargain with others for entry into their market on a basis of equality, scrupulously refusing to use their power to influence their smaller and weaker partners as Platt has argued [146; 148: 308f.]?

Peru appears to provide a most obvious example of anti-imperialist claims. At no time did the British attempt to gain any exclusive trading privileges, but were satisfied by a fairly liberal, non-discriminatory tariff treaty with legal safeguards for their nationals. The loans which British subjects made to Peru were defaulted on almost immediately, but the government in London would take no action except to offer a mild diplomatic mediation on the bondholders' behalf. In 1849, when repayments were resumed on the 1822 loan the initiative was taken almost entirely by the Peruvians, who wanted to clear their debts in order to make it easier for them to borrow again on the London market. The autonomy of Peru was demonstrated in other ways. Tariffs were persistently raised after 1830 (though not in a discriminatory fashion) despite repeated protests from British interests. The government also claimed a monopoly of the export of guano and exacted high prices from the British consumer; and the Peruvian government's hold over some of the British traders was used as a lever to extract loans out of them at favourable rates of interest. In none of these cases did the British feel any strong inclination to intervene [128; 129; 130; 131].

British relations with Argentina exhibit many similar features [37]. It is true that Popham, the British naval commander, decided in 1806 on his own initiative to claim the River Plate area for Britain and to discriminate against foreign imports. But he was soon disavowed and as early as 1807 Castlereagh was arguing that the only sensible policy was to encourage the growth of independence there and to negotiate for as free an entry into their markets as was possible by diplomatic means [38: ch. 1]. Later, a Spanish offer of commercial privileges for Britain in Latin American markets in return for political support against the rebels [38: *93*] could not tempt the British away from Castlereagh's policy which was formalised in the liberal Anglo-Argentinian treaty of 1825. As in Peru, there were rapid defaults on loans overenthusiastically subscribed in the aftermath of the treaty but the British would not intervene to enforce payment. Even the rise to power of Rosas, who was suspicious of European power and influence and who was inclined to protectionism, did not initially perturb them [38: chs 4-7].

Brazil, which was initially a part of the Portuguese empire, presented a rather different picture. Portugal was entirely dependent on Britain for her political survival, and in the eighteenth century the British had exploited this dependence to gain a predominance in Portuguese markets. In 1810, in return for further support, the Portuguese élite allowed the British into Brazilian markets. A low and discriminatory tariff concession was offered, together with certain privileges in shipping, and extraterritorial rights of jurisdiction were granted to British residents. These privileges were confirmed in 1827, when the Brazilians finally broke free of Portugal, the price they had to pay for Britain's support for their independence [174: *127f.*; 122: *71f.*]. The treaties effectively took away Brazil's tariff autonomy and forced her to keep duties low, while for their part the British penalised Brazil's major exports of coffee and sugar with high duties and gave their own colonies preferences in these commodities. In 1842, when the treaty came up for renewal the British, who had agreed on the extension of their privileges to other nations, offered some tariff concessions but basically wanted to retain the old unequal relationship. The Brazilians refused, the treaty lapsed and British privileges disappeared including the extraterritorial judicial rights which were abolished in 1845 [122: *281-98*]. Brazil's own position in the British market was made more favourable thereafter as colonial preferences were abolished.

At the same time that their privileges in Brazil were being eradicated the British were dabbling in politics elsewhere. The late 1830s and 1840s were an anxious time for British trade; traditional markets seemed stagnant and insecure. A Memorandum from the Board of Trade in 1840 reminded their government colleagues that new markets were required and that, in places like Latin America, it might be well worth while to take a more active part in supporting those regimes which were of a liberal cast and opposing those which were not. It was probably ideas such as this which prompted Britain to support Rosaria against Rosas in the struggle for control of Uruguay in the 1840s. The policy was never unwaveringly pursued and the Anglo-French naval attack on Montevideo in 1845 was a fairly half-hearted affair. It achieved nothing and the interventionist policy was soon dropped [38: ch. 9; 197: *100–8*]. The attempted penetration of Paraguay, which was prompted by the same fervour for opening up new markets, also faded out when it was realised that the potential of the area was very limited [95]. Similar worries about markets prompted an interest in free trade treaties with Texas in the 1840s but the policy failed and Texas was absorbed into the USA [195: *245–51*].

After 1850, these few attempts at privilege and control came to seem totally unnecessary as the élites of Latin America organised their countries and their constitutions in such a way as to develop trade contacts with Britain to the full and to encourage the British to invest in their lands for developmental purposes [38: ch. 10]. Platt claims, with some justice, that this relationship was not an imperialist one [150]. Graham, on the other hand, has argued that the determination of countries like Brazil and Argentina to model their economic life so closely on Britain's is in itself an imperialist triumph for the latter. This cultural imperialism – the acceptance of the aims and aspirations, norms and methods of a dominant nation by another less powerful one – is, he believes, the most complete form of imperialism if only because it is so inexpensive. Interference, as the British learned slowly in Brazil and Argentina, bred resentment and imperilled this relationship of dependence [65; 66].

(ii) INFORMAL EMPIRE IN THE FAR EAST

After 1815, the major problem facing Britain in China was the obstinate refusal of the Peking government to offer more than a very limited contact through Canton via the East India Company which retained its monopoly of the China trade. Opposition to the monopoly from private traders grew rapidly, and the East India Company's privileges here largely disappeared in 1833; but the freeing of the trade only helped to increase the impatience of British traders with their narrow Cantonese bridgehead at a time when export markets were hard to find. This, together with attempts by the Chinese to stem the outflow of silver by restricting the import of opium, led to war with Britain between 1839 and 1842. War broke out again between 1858 and 1860 when the British felt that the Chinese were placing unnecessary and insulting obstacles in the way of trade, infringing British rights. The results of the two wars were treaties which gave extraterritorial rights, opened up a number of Chinese ports and gave Britain sovereignty over Hong Kong and Kowloon which served as British trading and naval bases [69].

The British government, though not the local trading community, soon lost its early optimistic belief in the potentialities of Chinese commerce. So, while merchants complained about their limited access to the interior and the obduracy of local officials, and while they called for the downfall of the Emperor's government and constantly demanded forceful methods to open up China further, the Foreign Office was reluctant to take notice [144]. During the Taiping Rebellion, the British had occasionally demanded further trading concessions as the price of their support. The creation of the Imperial Maritime Customs in 1855 which put Chinese tariff policy finally under British control was one consequence of this [185: 237–50, 312–16]. Increasingly, though, the British felt that, apart from enforcing the existing treaty provisions, their main interest lay in supporting the existing government at Peking for fear that its collapse might bring anarchy, ruin trade and encourage foreign intervention [144: esp. 31]. Especially after 1860, the British adopted a very cautious approach to trade negotiations which led to only a very slow prising open of the Chinese oyster. Traders complained bitterly but they had to accept very limited advances, such as the Chefoo Convention of 1876 which increased the number of trading ports and made some other marginal changes. Meanwhile they continued to frighten themselves with nightmares about foreign intrusion and dreamed of a British empire in China or grand railway schemes which would connect Burma with the yet untapped (and largely imaginary) riches of Southern China. To all this, the Foreign Office maintained a polite indifference [144: 71–149].

In the mid-nineteenth century the penetration of Chinese markets was indeed small and trade grew very slowly. The Chinese, in fact, would not collaborate with the British except in the most minimal way and since the British government refused to push them very hard for fear of bringing about political collapse, Britain had no commercial hegemony worth speaking of, despite her dominance of Chinese trade [28; 57: 10]. Even Marx, after initially assuming that a collapse of the China trade might precipitate social revolution in Britain, came to recognise that the British had made little headway in the China market [2: 67–75, 393–8].

Attitudes to Japan were strongly influenced by the Chinese experience, and particularly the growing conviction by the 1850s that Oriental markets had been over-rated in importance. The first official attempt to breach Japan's self-imposed isolation was made only in 1855 and negotiations were largely confined to naval matters arising out of the Crimean War and fear of Russian use of Japanese ports [6: ch. 5]. The Elgin Treaty, signed in 1858, opened some ports to trade, defined low customs duties on a most-favoured nation basis and allowed for extraterritorial jurisdiction for British subjects [6: ch. 7]. As in China, the British were always anxious to get other powers with trading connections involved before acting on infringements of treaty rights. On this basis, naval power was used against Japan in 1863 and 1864 to defend foreign lives and property [27: 292–3]. In 1865, however, Parkes, the British chargé d'affaires seems to have gone further and organised a joint naval action to persuade the Shogun to make further tariff concessions and allow Japanese to trade more freely with Westerners [27: 297–9]. The British were none the less careful to support the central authority as an alternative to anarchy [45: 75–7, 94–6], and in the struggle between the Shogunate and their opponents, which ended in the Meiji Restoration of 1868, the British only shifted their support to the insurgents when the Shogun's power had obviously collapsed and the new men had shown themselves responsive to Western attitudes and demands [27].

Siam, if not as impenetrable as Japan was, like China, inclined to look with disfavour on foreign contacts in the early nineteenth century. The East India Company would have liked trading relations with Siam but trod warily for fear of involving itself in further responsibility and expense. The private traders, for their part, were more inclined to argue for a show of force to bring the Siamese to heel, especially after the Chinese War of 1839–42. A commercial treaty, signed in 1826, gave Britons the right to reside in Siam and to trade freely, irrespective of state monopolies. By the 1840s, these rights were being seriously infringed and, in response to complaints, the Foreign Office reluctantly sent Sir James Brooke of Sarawak fame to re-negotiate the treaty in 1850.

Brooke's initial reaction was that the British should proceed gently and wait for the heir apparent, Mongkut, to succeed to the throne since he was plainly more favourable to Western ideas than his predecessors. Unfortunately an insulting reception soon had him claiming that the Siamese needed a taste of the Chinese medicine and that the British ought to use their influence to place Mongkut on the throne immediately. The Foreign Office, who were aware of no overwhelming demand for Siamese markets, decided that his first advice was the best [184: 134–73]. Mongkut succeeded in 1851, and in 1855 signed a treaty which gave extended rights of residence, extraterritoriality and very favourable tariffs [184: *174–232*]. Siam's reactions, like Japan's suggest that they were influenced not simply by fear but also by admiration for British power and the desire to emulate it.

(iii) STRATEGY AND ECONOMIC POWER IN THE OTTOMAN EMPIRE

Britain's interest in the Ottoman Empire after 1815 was a complex one. The desire to check the expansion of Russia and prevent that power from threatening the lines of communication between Europe and the Near and Middle East went together with the need to protect markets in Turkish possessions. The biggest setback to these strategic and economic aims came in 1833 when, as a result of internal weaknesses, the Sultan signed a treaty with Russia which appeared to give the latter political paramountcy in his dominions. In the long diplomatic battle which Britain then undertook to regain lost ground, economic and political weapons were used in closely interlinked ways.

·The 1838 Anglo-Turkish Convention was the keystone of the policy. All the internal monopolies which had hitherto hindered trade in Turkey were removed and replaced by a modest non-discriminatory tariff on imports. It was expected that the boost to trade and development which this would bring would be to the advantage not only of Britain's exports but, by bringing into being a liberal middle class in Turkey, would prompt reforms which would make the state a more effective block against the pretensions of the autocratic and protectionist Russians. The British also tried to erect other barriers to the advancement of Russia in the Danubian provinces of the Ottoman Empire. They attempted to foster the grain trade there as a rival to Russia by breaching the Navigation Acts in 1838 and allowing the Austrians to export wheat from the Danube basin in their own ships, a privilege which was extended to the Austrian province of Galicia in 1842 [154: *78f, 119f., 142–3, 185*].

As a result of the workings of the Convention of 1838, the British superseded the Russians as the chief trading partner of Turkey and, by 1850, Turkey had become Britain's third biggest European customer [106; 154: *108–9*]. The growing grain trade with eastern Europe, together with the markets and supplies which Turkey provided, meant that an increasingly important direct economic interest in Turkey was added to Britain's strategic interest in maintaining the integrity of the ailing empire, and was in itself something to fight for in 1854 when

32

Britain and France went to war in defence of Turkey against Russia [154: *213–14*].

For the Turks, the Convention – which together with other agreements took away their tariff autonomy and forced them to accept low duties – meant a decline of local industry under pressure of British competition [106]. It also meant a greater difficulty in raising budgetary revenue and from 1854 onwards they borrowed heavily, especially from Britain and France, and thus became yet more economically dependent [154: *104–5*]. The importance of Turkey in British eyes can be gauged from the fact that the 1854 loan received the informal support of the British and French governments, the 1855 loan – a war loan – was guaranteed by them and later Turkish loans were also given public support by the British government [8: *48–54*].

In the 1830s and 1840s, as defenders of the integrity of the Ottoman Empire, the British were inevitably brought into conflict with Mehemet Ali, the ambitious pasha of Egypt, whose growing power seemed to threaten the stability of the empire and whose state monopolies offended liberal trading notions. Strong diplomatic pressure was applied to force Mehemet to abandon his monopolies and, when he clashed with and defeated the Sultan's army, Britain and Russia, who equally distrusted Mehemet, joined together in 1841 to use naval and military force to quell his ambitions [141: *199–201*; 61: *57–62*].

Persia was also important to Britain as a buffer against Russian advance in Central Asia which might pose a threat to control of India. As in Turkey, the British offered a dose of liberal commerce, intended to increase Britain's presence locally and raise indigenous collaborators, aided by occasional use of more forceful tactics. The commercial treaty, signed with Persia in 1841 for example, which gave low tariffs and most-favoured nation status to Britain, was only brought to a successful conclusion by a show of force [61: *20–3*].

Policy towards Turkey's tractable vassal, Morocco, was less forceful. The main concern here was to stem the flow of French influence from the adjacent colony of Algeria. As in Turkey, British policy was designed to counteract the danger of foreign penetration by extending commercial freedom. The Sultan of Morocco agreed to a treaty in 1856 which liberalised trade. Palmerston would have followed this up in 1861 by guaranteeing a loan to the Sultan. This proposal was vetoed; but the guarantee was given a year later by indirect, but equally effective, means [44: *165–181, 205–6, 211–12*].

5 Extensions of Formal Control 1815–75

IN the sixty years after the Congress of Vienna the area of the globe under British sovereign control expanded considerably. Gallagher and Robinson imply that these extensions of formal control were always undertaken, deliberately and for economic motives, when informal means of influence proved inappropriate. For his part, Platt denies that the movement of the imperial frontier was inspired by metropolitan ambition, preferring to argue that expansion was primarily undertaken for local reasons which might have an economic component. As might be expected, the picture which emerges from a close study of frontier expansion is rather more complicated than either party allows.

There are some examples of expansion which do seem to be the direct result of 'turbulent frontiers' where the 'man on the spot' took matters into his own hands and forced upon a reluctant home government an extension of its responsibilities [47]. The occupations of Sind and the Punjab on the North-West Frontier of India in 1843 and 1849 respectively are good instances of this [61: *48–51, 72–5*]. In the case of Burma, the annexation of territory there by the British in 1824 was the direct result of a frontier dispute in which the Burmese were the aggressors; while the further extension of control over Burmese territory in 1852 appears to have been a classic instance of a high-handed Indian viceroy, Dalhousie, using a trivial commercial dispute as an excuse to extend the frontiers of the empire in India [177: *1–25*; 14: *73–4, 86–8, 104–5*].

In these cases there were little or no British economic interests to encourage or protect. Even here, though, it must be remembered that the ultimate rationale of these frontier movements was the defence of India, an economic asset of primary importance. It is also of interest that the British did initially try to solve the problem of turbulence on the North-West Frontier by signing free-trade treaties with local groups which would, hopefully, put them firmly into Britain's economic orbit [61: *32*]. Besides which, the economic importance of Burma to Britain was growing steadily towards the end of the period. Treaties signed in 1862 and 1867 abolished state monopolies, allowed for extraterritorial rights and liberalised customs duties; they were a sign of Britain's growing interest in Burma as a market and as a key transit point on the road to the supposedly rich markets of south-west China. In this way, economic and strategic reasons for ensuring that Burma remained free of foreign interference became increasingly intertwined [163: ch. 4].

There are also a number of frontier extensions clearly attributable to changes in local economic conditions which required adjustments of political control as a consequence [72: *1–28*]. The creation of the Australian state of Queensland in the late 1850s was the result of migration out of the existing settlement of New South Wales and was eventually recognised as justifying the creation of a new state [104]. British Columbia was annexed in 1858 to counteract the influence of the gold-seeking American migrants who threatened to bring the government of the USA into an area adjacent to the existing Canadian colonies [62]. The incorporation of New Zealand in 1840 was in response to persistent claims from missionaries that white traders were disrupting Maori society bringing war, disease and social and political chaos [193: *75f.*, *98f.*; 194: *49–55*]. A similar breakdown of law and order under the impact of Western economic penetration occurred in Fiji. By 1870, white settlers had assumed political leadership there but they could not keep order amongst themselves nor could they prevent the growing abuses of the traffic in Polynesian labour sent to work on plantations in Australasia and other Pacific islands. The British government finally took over Fiji with extreme reluctance, in 1874 [116: chs 7, 11; 193: *238–66*].

In West Africa, constant disputes between British traders and African middlemen led to conflicts which slowly pushed British authority into the hinterland after 1850. Extension of control meant increasing local expense which itself led to high tariffs and continuous attempts by local British rulers to increase the area within which revenue could be raised [73: *41–5*, *58–62*; 140]. Despite the determination of the British government in the 1860s to halt 'creeping imperialism' [73: *64f.*; 116: *99–101*] the frontier continued to move inland, and attempts to rationalise and consolidate colonial possessions there, by swapping the Gambia for French territories nearer to Britain's Niger possessions, foundered because of the opposition of British business interests [116: *104–9*; 73: *151–5*]. Finally, war between the Ashanti and the British persuaded a reluctant Colonial Office to agree to the extension of control over the Gold Coast in 1874, in order to provide the security without which trade could not flourish. It has been claimed that the Gold Coast was annexed in a more positive spirit of economic enterprise but that view has yet to be clearly substantiated [116: chs 4, 9; 156: *95*].

In these instances, the economic changes which were bringing

35

political disruption were often too small or remote to arouse much interest in Britain herself. In the case of British Columbia and New Zealand it took the threat of foreign intervention to precipitate action in London; and in Fiji and British Columbia determined local officials played a large part in persuading the government to extend its authority.

Some extensions of the empire in this period were, therefore, undoubtedly the result of frontier problems to which British governments had to respond, however unwillingly. It is equally certain, though, that a number of areas were acquired very deliberately for reasons which were either straightforwardly economic, or where the economic element in policy making was of some considerable importance. Berar and Nagpur were added to the Indian empire in the 1840s because they were potentially very important suppliers of raw cotton [136: *160–5*]. Besides this, the British took control of a number of small coastal territories across the globe which were expected to perform a complex economic function.

Singapore was occupied by the British in 1819 and was subsequently developed by them as a free port, both to give an additional commercial-cum-naval base which could protect the growing trade between Britain, India and China, and to counteract Dutch attempts to extend their formal control and protectionist policies in South-East Asian waters. The acquisition of the port and its subsequent growth were crucial in establishing British economic paramountcy in the Malay Peninsula and ensuring control of the Malacca Straits, both of which were recognised by the Dutch in the treaty of 1824 which defined spheres of influence in the area. As Singapore grew, it steadily became the outstanding entrepôt for trade in the whole area providing at one and the same time both increasing markets for Britain and asserting and extending her naval and political predominance [124; 64: *339–42*; 163: *30f.*]. The extension of control to the port of Labuan on the North Borneo coast in 1846 was intended to fulfil the same objectives. Agreements with the Dutch on liberal trading provisions in the archipelago had become a dead letter by the 1840s and, with the stimulus of commercial depression behind them, the British hoped to counteract Dutch influence in the area by developing Labuan both as a naval coaling station and as a commercial entrepôt. In this case, the policy failed to produce the desired economic results [183: *83–7*; 184: *22–3*; 64: *384–5, 387–90, 393–401*; 26: *146, 148–50*].

The occupation of Aden in 1839 was also part of a deliberate strategy in which political, strategic and economic elements were all combined.

Here, the central concern was to bring law and order to the Persian Gulf and to keep hostile powers out of an area which was regarded as vital to the defence of the whole chain of Britain's economic and political commitments stretching from the Mediterreanean through the Ottoman Empire to India and other Far-Eastern markets and territories. Local sheikhs were steadily brought together to suppress piracy and liberate trade, and Egyptians, Turks and Persians were successfully kept away from the Gulf at different times, occasionally by force [92: *19–33*]. But the crucial move was the occupation of Aden. As trade grew, the British felt the need for a coaling station on the Gulf. Aden was also the focal point for the trade of its hinterland, the control and development of which would enhance British wealth and prestige; and it was an excellent base for wider naval operations as it straddled a major route to India [64: *294–305*; 59: ch. 1]. Lagos had a similar role in the more limited arena of West Africa where the British were determined to eliminate the slave trade and support legitimate commerce [56; 30: *203–4*]. In 1851, the British replaced the ruler and provided him with a resident adviser. Ten years later they went further and annexed the port intending to use it as a base from which to attack the slave trade, provide a presence which would uphold pliable local chiefs, and act as a focal point for the expansion of the palm-oil trade [73: *31–8, 53–6*]. Hong Kong (1841) and Kowloon (1861) were expected to perform the same function in relation to their British trade with China.

The steady incorporation of these small coastal bases into the British empire between 1815 and 1875 suggests that there was an organic connection in the minds of British statesmen between commercial expansion and strategic and naval defence. The bases provided means for the spread of trade in their hinterlands, strengthening Britain's hold on the interested friendship of the local political authorities and increasing her global prestige and power. In doing so, these small territories helped to satisfy economic and political needs without involving too much expense or administrative tedium – both of which were important considerations to a nation suspicious of government and keen to keep down public expenditure.

In a few instances of formal extensions of rule in this period it is difficult to assess which of the three categories of expansion mentioned above actually applies. In South Africa, where the fundamental British interest was in the Cape and its naval base, the political frontier was constantly extended in a vain attempt to maintain control over the Boers as they battled with the Bantu for land. This may be taken as a classic instance of a turbulent frontier where local governors were often provoked into extending control despite contrary instructions from a cheese-paring Parliament [49; 137: *152–71, 177f.*]. The movement of the frontier can, however, be interpreted differently. Atmore and Marks have claimed that the overriding British interest was in trying to persuade the Boers to settle down as capitalist farmers and thus become assimilated into the British-dominated Cape economy. The Boers refused to collaborate and moved away from British influence, the British in their turn following them, remorselessly pushing forward the political frontier to prevent the Boers from establishing an independence and being particularly careful to keep them away from the coast. For this reason, Britain annexed Natal in 1842. When the Boers crossed the Orange River in the 1850s and settled there, the British finally decided to pursue them no more, not because they were reconciled to Boer independence but because it was recognised that the small Dutch republics were landlocked and that the process of capitalist assimilation had begun. Once economic control was asserted, political control could be correspondingly relaxed [3: *120f.*].

Policy towards the Malay States has also been interpreted in sharply contrasted ways. The occupation of Singapore and agreements with the Dutch helped to concentrate British economic interests in the Malay Peninsula. Although the British in the shape of the East India Company occupied only four small points on the coast, they had a widespread interest in the hinterland. As early as the 1820s, the agents of the Company were meddling in the affairs of the Malay States, often without authority, suppressing piracy and trying to create the conditions in which commerce could flourish [184: *55f.*; 183: *76–9*]. An early interest was also shown in educating the local rulers to become better collaborators with British business. The great success here was Johore, where the ruler, enthusiastically supported by the British, created a strong government after 1862 which gave commercial interests no cause for complaint [191: *175*]. In the rest of Malaya, after 1850, matters were very different. As the mining and export of tin increased in importance, so the political structure of the states proved unable to cope with the strains economic progress brought with it. The wealth from the tin gave the established rulers' rivals the chance to threaten them and undermine political stability. European merchants exacerbated this by backing rival claimants in the hope of exclusive concessions; and the Chinese, who flocked into Malaya to mine tin, brought with them their secret-society conflicts which became bewilderingly entangled in the other struggles. As early as the 1860s, local

British officials were calling on their superiors to intervene decisively to restore law and order. Both the Company and the Colonial Office, which took over responsibility for Peninsula policy in 1867, evaded this crisis for as long as possible for fear of extending British responsibility permanently [191; 116: ch. 5].

The sending of residents to advise the rulers in states where law and order had broken down in 1874 can be seen merely as the final, reluctant recognition of a frontier problem, in which fear of foreign intervention and the forceful personality of the local British agent, Sir Andrew Clarke, played a decisive role in prompting action [26: *163–75*; 116: *205–9*; 5: *177–80*; 22]. It has been maintained, on the other hand, that the British intervened to foster commerce in Malaya for its own sake. From this point of view, the most important cause of intervention was the fact that American and European competition in South-East Asia was growing rapidly. British traders and businessmen were increasingly inclined to offset this by extending their contacts with the tin-producing states of the Peninsula, and required political backing there to safeguard their investments. In this interpretation, the invocation of a foreign menace by the Colonial Office is seen merely as a device to provoke the British Cabinet into an action the ultimate aim of which was to make Malaya safe for capitalism [97; 163: ch. 5].

6 Economics and Imperialism 1815–75

THE picture which emerges from this survey of the evidence of British economic imperialist activities in the period is more complex and fragmentary than any of those suggested in chapter 1. After 1815, a protectionist policy which included a deliberate strategy of colonialism was steadily modified until free trade became the order of the day. Free trade was frequently associated with a distaste for imperialism, and it can be argued that the political emancipation of the white colonies and the liberal nature of economic policy towards Latin American states exhibit this growing inclination to anti-imperialism. At the same time, it must be remembered that British control over and economic penetration of India was enlarged after 1815; and the evolving ideas of liberality of commerce in Britain did contain a strongly imperialist element, though economic hegemony rather than political control became the centre of discussion. The long-running conflict between those who associate free trade with the decline of the forces making for imperialism in Britain and those who see it merely as a device which allowed for a more subtle form of domination is particularly marked in the debate over British policy in Latin America, and it is evident also in the discussions about the growth of responsible government in the white colonies. Whether these areas were subject to informal control is a vexed question; in other parts of the world forms of domination are less difficult to discern. In China the role of force in imposing freer trade is clear, and less obvious forms of coercion were used to further British commercial interests elsewhere [cf. 178: 547]. In the Ottoman Empire, Siam, Japan and Morocco – where the British representative adopted a 'masterful tone' in the trade negotiations of the 1850s [44: 253] – fear of British power was an important element in gaining commercial concessions. The purpose behind this determination to extend liberal trading was often, of course, the desire to extend markets, but there was also interaction between widening the area for trade and strategic and military needs. Sometimes, for example, the British were more interested in keeping an area out of the clutches of another great power than they were in promoting a trade of importance to the metropolis. In these instances, the introduction of free trade was seen as a means of encouraging economic ties which would inspire development locally and keep sensitive areas out of the economic orbit of rival powers. Policy towards China is a good example of a straightforward interest in trade expansion. Relations with Texas and Morocco exemplify the latter type of strategy; while policy in the Ottoman Empire was often nicely balanced between the two.

The rationale behind extensions of formal control was also varied. There was a tendency for frontiers to move in spite of the expressed wishes of British governments and, since the 'men-on-the-spot' were often of aristocratic or military extraction, there is a strong element of truth in the contemporary radical and Schumpeterian claim that the forces making for expansion were pre-capitalist in nature. The extension of British power on the North-West Frontier and the acquisition of part of Burma in 1852 seem explicable in these terms. Yet it is clear that the turbulence out of which frontier movements arose was often caused by economic upheavals related ultimately to changes in the world economy of which Britain was the centre. The acquisition of British Columbia is the best instance of this. Again, some additions to empire were made with deliberation and planned or at least encouraged in London. In the case of Berar, Nagpur, Singapore, Lagos or Labuan, to take the prime examples, the pressure for trade expansion determined their occupation. Strategic motives were uppermost when Aden was absorbed yet, here again, the idea was that Aden might act as a fulcrum for trade in its hinterland, underlining the British presence by extending economic control. There are also a number of important extensions of formal control – in South Africa, Malaya and West Africa – where the desire to increase trade may have played an important part in encouraging the British government to act.

A relationship between an emergent free trade strategy and formal and informal imperialism did exist between 1815 and 1875 to some degree. This suggests a much closer look at the connections between changes in the growth and direction of British foreign trade and overseas investment (which became rapidly more important after 1850) and imperial activity than has been attempted hitherto. Platt has argued that the slow growth of British foreign trade between 1815 and 1850 indicates a domestically centred economy with little interest in overseas expansion. On the other hand, it might be the case, as Wakefield and Marx believed (and as a study of the growth of free trade ideas suggests) that the sluggish growth of foreign trade was a vexing problem which could, from time to time, provoke an interest in imperial expansion. As a brief indication of the possibilities let us consider Table 1.

Table I

Exports of British Produce by Area 1816–42 (£m. current prices: quinquennial averages)

	1816–20	1838–42	% change 1816–20 to 1838–42
North Europe	11·4	12·8	+12
South Europe	7·3	9·5	+30
Africa	0·4	1·7	+325
Asia	3·4	7·9	+132
USA	7·0	6·5	−7
British North America and West Indies	7·0	5·8	−31
Foreign West Indies	1·0	1·1	+10
Central and Southern America	2·8	5·4	+93
Total Exports	40·3	50·5	+25

Data Source: A. H. Imlah, *Economic Elements in the Pax Britannica* (1958) p. 129.

The table indicates that between the end of the Napoleonic Wars and the 1840s, Britain was finding it extremely difficult to increase exports or even maintain them in terms of current prices in European and North American markets. Elsewhere, markets were expanding rapidly: some 80 per cent of the total increase in the value of trade arose in Africa, Asia and Latin America. Furthermore, in the 1830s and 1840s the British went to war with China, signed the Anglo-Turkish Convention, occupied Aden, took a more robust attitude to Latin American involvements and showed an increasing interest in Wakefieldian schemes for colonial development. Whether the correlation between the changing structure of overseas markets and formal and informal expansion overseas is significant or not is a question which should, perhaps, become the central one in the debate over the next few years.

Part II 1875–1914

7 Economic Background and Theoretical Approaches

AFTER 1875 the British economy, although growing in absolute terms, was in relative decline compared with other great powers, notably the USA and Germany. Not only had these countries become larger producers of manufactures by 1900, but in many important sectors of industry they had taken a significant technological lead over the first industrial nation. Britain's relative decline was reflected in a more sluggish rate of growth of exports than hitherto and a sharp fall in Britain's share of world trade. Competition became fiercer not only overseas but even in Britain's domestic market; at the same time, although Britain retained free trade, the trend towards commercial liberalism in the rest of the world, apparent before the 1870s, was arrested. Imports rose faster than exports and the deficit on balance of commodity trade grew considerably. This deficit would have been much greater but for the buoyancy of trade with the empire. While total exports at current prices increased by only 6 per cent between 1871–5 and 1896–1900, exports to the empire rose by 29 per cent and the increase in sales to the white settled areas within the empire was 45 per cent.* These figures must be kept in mind when assessing, first, the significance of the reviving interest in closer economic unity with the empire, especially the white-settled parts, after 1875 and the clamour to abandon free trade; and, secondly, the business agitation for the incorporation of large areas of Africa and Asia into the formal empire in this period.

Besides growing imperial markets, the other great offset to Britain's declining competitiveness abroad was the rapid growth of her income from services such as shipping and overseas loans. Britain compensated for her relatively low level of domestic investment in this period by sending substantial amounts of her capital abroad. The export of capital which first became a prominent feature in the mid-century

* Calculated from figures in B. R. Mitchell and P. Deane, *Abstract of British Historical Statistics* (1962), sect. xi; and *The Statistical Abstract of the UK*. The white colonies are British North America, Australia, New Zealand, the Cape of Good Hope and Natal.

43

reached enormous proportions by the turn of the century and returns on these investments took on a prime significance as the balance of commodity trade gap widened (see Table II).

Table II
Balance of Payments on Current Account (£m.)

	Balance of Commodity Trade	Shipping Income	Interest, Profits, Dividends	Other Invisibles	Balance of Payments on Current Account
1871–5	−64	+51	+83	+5	+75
1896– 1900	−159	+62	+132	+5	+40

Data Source: P. Deane and W. A. Cole, *British Economic Growth 1688–1959* (1962) p. 36.

In view of the rising importance of income from investments abroad it is not surprising that contemporaries suggested an intimate connection between capital export and the very rapid increase in British formal control in parts of Africa and Asia in this period. J. A. Hobson argued in *Imperialism. A Study* that severe maldistribution of income was placing large amounts of capital in the hands of a financial class who needed secure overseas markets to safeguard these investments. The battle between the powers for these markets for capital led, he believed, both to extensions of empire and also to a desire to protect these markets from foreign competition [81: esp. *71–93*]. One immediate difficulty with Hobson's argument is that there is very little correlation between the areas acquired by Britain after 1870 – mainly in Africa and Asia – and the markets for overseas loans which were mainly white-settled areas such as Latin America, the white colonies and other parts of the empire [40: *54–60*]. On the other hand, it has been argued that the Hobsonian approach can be applied by taking note of the crucial significance of the relatively small amounts of capital – such as that invested in chartered companies, for instance – in helping Britain to attain control in certain areas of Africa and Asia [111].

Later, Marxist writers emphasised capital export as crucial to expansion [4]. Luxemburg claimed that the export of capital to areas outside the capitalist environment was vital to the survival and growth of the system which would otherwise collapse under the strain of over production and falling rates of profit. Lenin adopted a subtler approach. He saw the expansion of European influence and empire in Africa and Asia before 1900 as part of the competitive search for markets for both trade and capital between the industrial powers. After 1900, there emerged monopoly capitalism dominated by finance which led to rapid increases in capital export and an attempt by the various imperialist states to redivide an already divided world [180; 96: ch. 1; 109].

Gallagher and Robinson have denied this connection between economic changes in Britain and Europe and overseas expansion [57: 12–15]. They have argued that there is little correlation between the major movements of trade and capital in this period and the territories actually acquired. They also point out that Britain maintained her free trade policy up until 1914. The extension of control was, instead, the results of changes outside Britain. First, the competition amongst the great powers for overseas markets, who were often protectionist in spirit, led the British to mark out areas in order to preserve them for free trade. Secondly, many of the areas hitherto informally controlled began to collapse, politically and economically, under the weight of British penetration and formal empire had to be accepted as a *pis aller*. The late Victorians were, the authors assert, no more overtly imperialist than their forbears but formal control was more often forced on them. Their fondness for informality can be gauged from the endless and often futile expedients which they devised to avoid the distasteful necessities of direct control. After 1880, according to Gallagher and Robinson, there was no new imperialism but only the increasing breakdown of an older policy of informality. Pursuing the theme of collaboration, Robinson later laid stress on the collapse of indigenous authority as the central cause of the scramble for territory after 1880, at the same time playing down the role of European imperialist rivalry. In doing so, he underlined his earlier belief in the continuity of aim and impulse from Britain throughout the century [159]. This emphasis on what he calls the 'peripheral' explanations of European expansion in the late nineteenth century is also characteristic of the work of D. K. Fieldhouse. The reason for the expansion of formal control was the collapse of governmental institutions, eroded by decades of Western penetration which reluctant European governments were forced to offset by direct rule [39; 40: chs 1–3. Cf. 182; 114: 236–9; 108].

Platt, in his attack on this argument, has reverted to a position closer to Hobson and the Marxists. The need for overseas markets and supplies increased rapidly after 1850 and the export of capital became a significant adjunct to trade relations. Traders and investors became increasingly fearful of the protectionist policies of other industrialising nations and the British government was exhorted by business interests to keep open the channels of trade. Hence the policy of anticipatory annexation in Africa after 1880, and the 'spheres-of-interest' policy in China and other areas which tried to ensure that the British should not be locked out of the battle for financial and economic concessions which threatened to pull these countries out of Britain's economic orbit. So, after 1880, both in areas of commercial importance and in those of strategic and military significance in relation to our overseas economic commitments, British officials could be found promoting individual firms or actively supporting the formation of British banks and syndicates, bringing pressure upon them to lend to foreign governments and protect the 'national interest'. Beginning after 1850 and reaching its climax after 1880 there is, according to Platt, a new imperialism, both formal and informal, which is a reflection of changing economic structures in Europe [148: *353f.*; 147; 153: *11–13*]. These varied arguments must now be tested against the evidence available about British expansion overseas after 1875.

8 Protectionism and Empire Unity after 1875

THE years after 1875 saw a growing interest in the idea of re-establishing some special economic relationship with the white colonies. Industrial difficulties were the base from which grew more comprehensive fears, gaining in strength as 1914 approached, that Britain, if she maintained free trade, was in danger of losing her industrial supremacy and her world-power status. Many academics, journalists and politicians, as well as businessmen, were impressed by the large, rapidly growing populations and resources of countries such as Germany and the USA; and it was not lost on them that these great powers had been consolidated and sustained behind protectionist barriers which gave them control of their own markets. Such speculations led on, naturally enough, to the idea that Britain should join with her white colonies – whose growth potential was reckoned to be enormous and who had a large appetite for British goods [151: *105–15*] – to create an economic and political unit of similar size and power, whose self-sufficiency would add to Britain's security and take her into the twentieth century assured of great-power status. For those with grand conceptions such as this, free trade seemed to offer only the prospect of increasing exclusion from overseas markets; the export of capital and manpower to our industrial rivals; and the fragmentation of the empire itself which would eventually be pulled into the economic orbit of larger, more rapidly growing industrial nations [35: ch. 5; 9:pts. II and III; 16].

The first political group which advocated the abandonment of free trade and closer economic unity with the empire were the Fair Traders whose strength, in the 1880s, lay in the embattled industries of wool, iron and agriculture [10; 199]. They advocated a tariff on manufactured imports partly as a retaliatory weapon against foreign protectionism and also proposed a 10 per cent to 15 per cent tariff on both manufactures and foodstuffs from foreign countries and free entry for empire commodities. In return, the Fair Traders hoped that empire countries would give Britain a preferential position in their markets [200: *136*]. But, despite this interest in imperial unity, it remains true that the Fair Traders were often more concerned to protect British industry and agriculture against all kinds of competition than they were to unite the British possessions overseas [10: *89–90*].

Fair trade – which only attracted mass support in times of acute depression and unemployment [10: *131f.*] – never had much chance of success. The British had signed treaties with foreign countries in the past in which they had voluntarily given up their right to preferential economic relations with their white colonies. Repudiation of these treaties invited the injured parties to retaliate [72: *77–9;* 192: *53f.*]; and, since two-thirds of our export trade actually went to areas outside the empire, the possibilities of injurious retaliation if Britain abandoned free trade seemed formidable [72: *81*]. It was also felt that, although the colonies were keen on preferences in the British market, they were protectionist in spirit and any concessions they were likely to offer in return would be unlikely to compensate Britain for the sacrifice of her commercial freedom [192: *170;* 10: *116–17*]. Even if the colonies did offer generous concessions, it was claimed that Britain's share of their import trade was often so large already that there was little further for her to gain [192: *60*]. Besides this, there was a widespread commitment to free trade as a cheap import policy. Any party which adopted a fair trade stance would be accused of advocating dearer food and damned in consequence.

The defence of free trade rested principally with the Liberals while the Conservative Party became increasingly doubtful about it as time passed. A fair trade motion was passed at the Conservative Conference in 1887 but the prime minister, Salisbury, ignored it because it invited electoral disaster [10: *65–74;* 192: *86*]. None the less, his government between 1886 and 1892, did begin to consider seriously whether it might be worthwhile to abandon free trade if a big enough concession was offered by the white colonies in return [189]. When Chamberlain became Colonial Secretary in 1895, the question of imperial economic unity began to move steadily to the centre of the political stage. Convinced that Britain's future standing in the world, if not her present wealth, depended upon closer relations with her white empire, Chamberlain first proposed an imperial Zollverein (free trade within the empire and a tariff against foreigners) in 1897. The idea got a cool reception. It offended not only free trade sentiment in Britain but also failed to impress the colonists. A Zollverein would have put their nascent industries at the mercy of Britain besides taking away their fiscal autonomy and chief source of revenue [72: *83–6;* 200: *140*]. Instead, the colonies proposed mutual preferences which would give them advantages in the British market while ensuring economic independence [10: *118f.*].

Once the Zollverein proposal was abandoned, Chamberlain cast about for more limited but effective means of unity. He repudiated British treaty obligations and allowed the colonies – first Canada, then later Australia and New Zealand – to offer us preferences in their markets in the hope of reciprocal concessions [72: *86–8*]. Chamberlain tried to provide the latter in 1902 when he argued that the small duty on corn imports imposed during the Boer War for revenue purposes should be retained only on foreign imports, thus allowing empire countries free entry. He failed to persuade the Conservative Cabinet that this preferential policy was correct, and subsequently left it to campaign for tariff reform and imperial reciprocity in 1903 [200: *144f.*].

Chamberlain's campaign was a deliberate attempt to reshape the Conservative Party and increase its electoral popularity. Tariff reform was intended not only as a means of initiating imperial economic unity but would also provide revenue for a programme of social reform and make it easier to meet rising defence costs as the possibilities of a conflict with Germany grew greater. Protection and preference were, therefore, key parts of a wider policy of 'social imperialism', designed to rally mass support for a policy of empire consolidation, in contradistinction to the Liberals' idea of maintaining free trade and cultivating less formal links with the white colonies [167: chs 4–7].

In the short run, Chamberlain's policy proved a severe handicap to the Conservative Party which was split on the tariff issue and badly beaten at the election of 1906. The tariff campaign was undoubtedly badly affected then and later by the fact that the export trade of Britain underwent a remarkable, if temporary, revival in the decade before the war. However, after the 1906 election, the Conservative rump was strongly protectionist and, from 1910, the party built up its electoral strength and the opposition to free trade became more formidable. None the less, like the Fair Traders, the tariff reformers as a body were often inclined to put protection above imperial preference and empire unity in their scale of priorities. Despite the original intention of Chamberlain, the Conservatives dropped the idea of tariffs on foreign food imports in 1913 because they feared the electoral implications of the 'dear loaf'. Free trade was dying but imperial economic unity was not its obvious heir when war broke out [167: *124–7*; 16].

9 Formal Empire in Africa and Asia

ROBINSON and Gallagher's explanation of Britain's part in the Scramble for Africa after 1880, which is still the dominating influence in the discussion, is an attempt to discredit the view that changing economic conditions in Europe had any important part to play in the drama. They claim that the proximate cause of the Scramble was the breakdown of informal influence in Egypt which made it necessary for the British to assume control there in order to safeguard the Suez waterway and the routes to the East. France's exclusion from what hitherto had been a joint financial control of Egypt led her to react violently against Britain in other parts of Africa. Other powers were drawn in and the stock market in African properties was under way. In the process, it is claimed, the British were reluctantly forced to acquire the whole of the Nile Valley as a means of securing their position at Suez. Similarly, they felt it necessary to consolidate their hold on the other area of strategic significance in Africa, the Cape, by going to war with the Boer republics, which the British believed were intent on removing South Africa from imperial control. In West Africa, an area which had economic but not strategic significance, the British asserted themselves on the Lower Niger, but elsewhere conceded large areas of territory, especially to the French, as useful pieces of bait in the diplomatic battle for strategic safety elsewhere in Africa.

In this view, it is crises on the periphery of empire leading to diplomatic complications in Europe and competition between the great powers which triggered off partition. Britain joined in with extreme reluctance and with an eye, not to African markets, but to the overall security of her Indian possessions. The partition, therefore, had little to do with any changes in the structure or performance of British industry and trade. The idea of developing African territories, which arose when Chamberlain became colonial secretary after 1895, is seen purely as a *post hoc* rationalisation of conquests undertaken for other reasons [157; 158].

The acquisition of the Nile Valley and Uganda in the 1890s seems to bear out Gallagher and Robinson's contentions. Although some interest was shown, in the 1880s, both in the Foreign Office itself and in business circles, in developing East African markets [18; 53: 26–7, 75,

87–8, 137], the government ignored it and was prepared to allow the Germans to make considerable territorial claims behind Zanzibar [157: *194–8;* 53: *94–106*]. In the late 1880s when the British became convinced that they would have to stay in Egypt for strategic reasons, control of the Nile Valley took on a new importance [157: *254–89;* 24: *119–22*]. It was strategy which prompted the British to agree to the creation of MacKinnon's chartered British East Africa Company as a means of asserting a presence in the Nile headwaters [53: *124–43;* 157: *198–202;* 24: *130*]. When the Company failed in 1892, the British reluctantly occupied Uganda formally [157: *307–30;* 24: *139–45*]. They completed their control of the area in 1898 by reoccupying the Sudan which had broken away from Egyptian control in the mid-1880s. There was a powerful lobby arguing for the need to safeguard Uganda as a future market [25: *434–6*]. Besides this, the strategic interest in the Sudan was to some extent subordinated, after 1894, to a growing jingoistic determination to humiliate the French; and this irrational drive does seem to have included a strong element of fantasy about future economic prospects in Africa [161: *392–403*]. The bulk of the evidence suggests, none the less, that the strategic importance of the Nile Valley in relation to the Mediterranean and India, was the most important determinant of policy in East Africa after 1880.

(i) ORIGINS OF THE SCRAMBLE

In their search for the origins of the Scramble, historians are now inclined to look back into the 1870s well before the Egyptian crisis. The boundaries of both French and British colonies in West Africa were expanding in the 1870s for reasons connected with economic changes in Europe (p. 50 above); and the continent was beginning to attract a lot of attention, some of it British, as a future source of wealth and trade, [179; 52]. It has also been argued that one of the precipitating causes of the partition was the ambition of Carnarvon, Disraeli's colonial secretary in the mid-1870s, to assert some sort of Monroe Doctrine over Africa [162: *22;* 63: *117*]. And, as early as 1878, the British had conceded paramountcy in Tunis to the French, in return for occupying Cyprus for strategic reasons, despite having previously competed with the French there for political and economic influence over the local rulers [125: *45–6, 57f.*].

Again, although free trade remained British policy until 1914, its maintenance does not necessarily imply, as Gallagher and Robinson appear to believe [57: *12*], that there was continuity in overseas economic policy. Gallagher and Robinson do not appreciate the extent to which, from the 1880s, business interests in Britain began to believe that large extensions of formal or informal control in Africa and Asia were compatible with free trade. Businessmen hitherto had tended to a cosmopolitan approach to international trade but, as competition for markets between the industrial powers increased rapidly and the profits of industry in Britain were squeezed, they began to take an interest in anticipatory annexation of overseas markets. The main fear was that large areas of the world might otherwise be occupied by rival powers with protectionist inclinations and 'far from being inconsistent with free trade, intervention in semi-civilized regions was regarded as an anti-cyclical measure for the restoration of commercial prosperity by a widening of the free trade area' [87: *975*. Cf. 147: *123f*; 179: *488*; 173: *1231–4*; 181: *183–6*; 86: *158–61*; 162: *10*].

(ii) THE OCCUPATION OF EGYPT IN 1882

Robinson and Gallagher's assumption here is that the financial problems of the khedive, who had borrowed extensively from European bankers, had brought on a crisis of authority in Egypt which had reduced that country to anarchy. With the safety of Suez in mind, the British, after many attempts to get joint action with other powers, had reluctantly intervened to counteract the collapse of informal rule [157: *155–9*; 158: *78–80*]. Platt is in general agreement with Robinson and Gallagher in this instance [148: *154f.*].

The notion that the British intervened to counteract hopeless internal disorder in Egypt is very questionable [142]. The khedive's bankruptcy had, by the late 1870s, placed the Egyptian economy under British and French control and this control appears to have been exercised in the interests of European investors and traders on the automatic assumption that this was also in the interests of the Egyptians [164: *779*; 141: *205–8*; 155: *113*]. In the process of reorganising the finances, the British financial controller placed high taxes on the local landed élite and also reduced the funds of the Egyptian army [155: *86f.*]. It was these groups – despising the khedive as a tool of the foreigner – who came together through the Chamber of Notables to object to aspects of the economic control and to claim the right to participate in economic and financial decision-making. As far as the British financial controllers were concerned, these claims threatened 'disorder and anarchy' [164: *777, 782*; 155: *96–7*]. In this biased form, the 'crisis' in Egypt came to the attention of the British government, already preoccupied with severe problems in Ireland. Eventually, the sympathy with which some members of the Liberal cabinet viewed the nationalist revolt in Egypt was eroded and Gladstone and Chamberlain came to believe that the country was ruled by military violence [19: *240–2*]. It also appears that, far from being a central concern from the beginning, the problem of Suez only came to prominence in British discussions about Egypt just before intervention in 1882, and even then, Suez was never thought to be as important as the Cape route [164: *778*; 19: *242*]. Egypt had for decades been increasingly drawn into the economic orbit of the West; and it can be argued that the occupation of 1882 was a means of overcoming the strains that this contact had imposed on the local political culture and ensuring that the country maintained an economic order which was agreeable to British and other European interests there [141: *208*].

(iii) WEST AFRICA AND THE CONGO

The belief that West African economic interests were subordinated to more important strategic considerations in the east of the continent has brought *Africa and the Victorians* [157] under fire from the beginning. Strong economic interests already existed in West Africa which made more effective claims on British governments than Robinson and Gallagher were willing to admit. The consensus of opinion appears to be that the extension of British control in West Africa had very little to do with the Egyptian crisis and its aftermath, that policy was largely dictated by commercial considerations and that the partition there 'may be regarded as a classic case study of commercial imperialism' [43: *93–4*].

As has already been shown (p. 52) the commercial crisis of the 1870s in Europe was giving both British and French colonialists in West Africa the incentive to expand the boundaries of their existing coastal enclaves. One effect of this was to create a deep-seated fear in both Britain and France about the local expansionist tendencies of the other, and to increase the desire for anticipatory annexation on both sides.

British fear of encroaching French imperialism and protectionism is obvious in the dispute over the Congo basin. As usual, the British were reluctant to undertake formal occupation, especially as existing trading interests there were small. None the less, there was powerful business pressure in Britain to keep the Congo free trading because of its supposed economic potential; the big worry was French occupation.

Hence the British proposed that Portugal, a small power over whom they had a strong influence, should occupy the Congo and, when that policy failed, fell back on support for Leopold, King of the Belgians, who also offered commercial liberalism [112; 113].

The central British concern at the Berlin Conference of 1884–5 which decided the fate of the Congo, was with the Niger [113: *177f.*]. Trade was already established there and, under stress of commercial depression and falling prices, businessmen weaved extravagant fantasies about the area's potential for trade and growth [75: *22f.*]. As fear of French ambition increased and traders on the coast became more interested in the control of economic activity in the interior, the British were constrained to declare a protectorate over the Oil Rivers area on the Nigerian Coast [30: *214*; 43: *107*; 157: *177–80*]. By the mid-1880s, too, Goldie, the leading British trader in the area, had established himself as the prime commercial power especially on the Middle Niger, control of which he regarded as overwhelmingly important to ensure the benefits for Britain of 'the only great remaining underdeveloped opening for British goods' [30: *210–11*]. It was to safeguard this area (in the cheapest manner available, of course) that the British government offered Goldie a charter for his Royal Niger Company in 1886 [42: *48ff.*]. And when agreements were made with the French between 1889 and 1891 on spheres of interest in West Africa, the lines drawn on the map were largely those favoured by Goldie and his fellow West African traders [74: *276–9*].

British expansion to safeguard trade was also sometimes precipitated by the collapse of native authority in the interior markets which served the coastal traders. The fall in the prices of traded products which began in the late 1870s had much to do with this. Indigenous leaders, formerly made powerful by the slave trade, had to rely on the more precarious revenue from palm oil once slavery was abolished. The fall in the price of palm produce further undermined their position to the point where social collapse began. The traders on the coast, themselves in straitened circumstances, and sometimes fearful of imperial control and imperial taxes, began to feel that the disorder in the interior must be quelled to safeguard trade. Under severe pressure from mercantile interests in Britain, and with an eye to the expansion of the French, the British government reluctantly pacified the Lagos hinterland and gave it protectorate status in the early 1890s [83: 1; 84; 85: ch. 4].

Moreover, as even Robinson and Gallagher were forced to admit [158: *114*], once Chamberlain came to exercise a decisive role in colonial policy after 1895, a very positive policy of acquisition in West

Africa was adopted. Some of the braggadocio of the Nile conflict with the French rubbed off on the West Coast too [74: *280–1*], and Chamberlain took control over the Ashanti and other areas to ensure openings there for British trade in the future [43: *110*]. Chamberlain was also interested in the idea, bitterly fought by the Treasury, of using state finance to build railways and other infrastructural investments which would bring these African territories into the world market [31]. At the end of the day, although it is true that the French commanded the lion's share of the territory in West Africa, the four British colonies which remained controlled 'the denser African populations, the larger productive capacities, and the preponderance of trade' [43: *111*].

(iv) SOUTHERN AFRICA

The conquest of the Boer republics by the British at the turn of the century was one of the events which provided J. A. Hobson with materials for his theory of finance capitalism. The war was, Hobson believed, supported by British statesmen like Milner and Chamberlain, on behalf of the great South African mining magnates, the profitability of whose investments in the Transvaal mines was threatened particularly by the refusal of President Kruger to organise black labour in the required manner [80].

Many historians have subsequently cast doubt on this interpretation and Robinson and Gallagher dismiss it entirely. They focus their attention on the strategic importance of the Cape which the British hoped to secure by encouraging the South African colonies to federate and form a strong self-governing dominion, as Canada had done in 1867. Carnarvon's disastrous attempt in the late 1870s apart [63: esp. *204–19*], the British were usually inclined to wait for federation to come about spontaneously and to put up with the Boer republics in the interior, who were hostile to British local paramountcy, because they were small and unimportant. What made this policy redundant was the discovery of gold in the Boer republic of the Transvaal in 1886. From penniless states, on the fringe of economic activity, the republics were transformed in a few years into the centre of economic life in South Africa. Thereafter, the British were worried lest the republics should become the focal point for a union of South Africa hostile to British paramountcy and a threat to the Cape. Policy was thus concerned with trying to absorb the Boers into a British federation and in encouraging Rhodes in his imperialist designs in Matabeleland and Mashonaland to the north in the hope that mineral discoveries there would provide a

55

British-dominated 'counterpoise' to the Transvaal [54; 55: esp. ch. 10]. Once Rhodes' chartered South Africa Company had failed in the north, the British fell back on the policy of pressurising the republic to enfranchise the mass of non-Boer immigrants whose votes would hopefully swing the Transvaal back into the British orbit of control. It was the failure of this strategy which led to war in 1899. The Jameson Raid of 1895 – when Rhodes led an unsuccessful foray to overthrow the Transvaal government – is seen only as a blundering local attempt to achieve Rhodes' 'imperial' ambitions and of no overriding importance [158: *117–24*; 157: *410–61*; 58].

In the last few years there have been some interesting attempts to examine the economic mainsprings of Rhodes' activity. Blainey has claimed that Rhodes and his confederates did have a direct economic interest in overthrowing Kruger in 1895. As deep-level miners they were in serious financial difficulties which were enhanced by the Transvaal government's uncooperativeness in organising the native labour supply and its dynamite monopoly. Rhodes, Blainey argues, had sound financial reasons for organising the Jameson Raid, while those mining magnates who did not join him were usually outcrop mine-owners with an assured profitability [7]. Since then, it has been claimed that Rhodes was financially secure in 1895 and that many of the mining magnates who were not, such as Barneto, had nothing to do with the Raid. Consequently, Kubicek claims, it is wrong to see the Raid as a mere rationalisation of economic need – vaguer 'imperialist' motives must also be taken into account [107]. It is certainly true that many of Rhodes' colleagues in the South Africa Company knew nothing of the Raid until it was over, and were extremely bitter about his part in it [51].

The connection between Rhodes' financial interests and his empire building continue to fascinate. Phimister has recently reasserted the idea that Rhodes had not been very successful on the Rand and that his imperial ambitions, as expressed through the chartered company, were largely motivated by the desire for gold. This was the reason for the suppression of the Matabele; and the 'failure of Chartered territory to provide immensely rich goldfields considerably accentuated Rhodes' interest in and dependence upon deep level mining' and gave him sufficient motive to plan the Raid in 1895 [145: *83, 86*].

Whatever the outcome of the discussion about the precise nature of the financial capitalists' sub-imperialist activities, it could still be claimed that metropolitan policy, both in licensing Rhodes' counter-poise and in pressurising Kruger into giving immigrants the vote, was dictated by the need to safeguard the Cape rather than a desire to make South Africa safe for capitalism. There are those, however, who would argue that British policy from 1870 onwards was motivated by a desire 'to establish a modern polity in South Africa – which would provide the necessary infrastructure for the maintenance and development of crucial British economic interests' such as gold production, and that this was the underlying, if not the proximate cause, of the Boer War [3: *128*]. From this angle, even if it cannot be proved that the post-1902 economy of South Africa was run directly in the interests of the mining capitalists [29; 132], it still remains true that the eventual settlement of the Union of South Africa in 1910 ministered both to strategic interests at the Cape and Britain's local and powerful economic interests [3: *127f.*].

(v) ECONOMIC IMPERIALISM IN SOUTH-EAST ASIA AFTER 1875

The importance of trading considerations in determining extensions of formal control in this part of the world has recently been reasserted. In the case of Upper Burma, for example, which was annexed in 1885, it has usually been claimed that the British only became keenly interested in formal control in 1884 when they believed the French might conclude a treaty with the Burmese which would undermine British authority in an area close to India [5: *181f.*]. Recent work suggests, however, that the importance of Burma as a route to the supposed wealth of south-west China and the direct interest in the growing teak trade were the guiding factors in policy. Annexation because of lack of co-operation from the Burmese authorities was considered as early as the 1870s but deferred because attention was diverted to problems elsewhere [177: *88–91*]. The occupation of Burma was finally precipitated by fear of French encroachment, but the British government was responding just as much to the clamour of business interests in Britain and South-East Asia as it was to fears for the defence of India [163: ch. 6; 87: *93–5*; 144: *149–52*].

Competition between pressure for markets and fields for investment and the overriding Foreign Office concern for the strategic defence of India is also evident in policy towards Siam. In London it was assumed that Siam's central importance was as a buffer state between Britain and France as Asian powers. The Siamese exercised a considerable degree of economic autonomy while adhering to the general principles of liberal trading which the British favoured and which was the best guarantee of that autonomy [11]. It was to defend this strategic interest based on informal economic power that the British government,

57

encouraged by business, warned the French off the Siamese heartland in 1893 and chivvied them into a mutual guarantee of this territory in 1896 [99]. As part of this policy, the British and Indian governments also assumed initially that the Siamese must be maintained as overlords of the four northernmost Malay states for fear that, if they fell to Britain, the Siamese would react by moving closer to France [186: *132–4*]. This did not suit the local British officials in Malaya who, in conjunction with local interests, had already absorbed Negri Sembilan and Pehang [186: *126–8*], and who were keen to further local industry and trade under the umbrella of British sovereignty [186: *123f.*]. Local pressure was sufficient to induce the British government to send residents to two of the northern states in 1902. After the Anglo-French *entente* of 1904, the Siamese also came to feel that they might be squeezed between these one-time enemies and therefore followed a policy of conciliating both by making concessions in areas where their own control was weak. Hence the British acquired, in 1909, the four northern Malay states which the local officials and business community had long coveted as markets [163: ch. 7; 100].

The extension of British control over North Borneo in the 1880s seems to have been agreed as a means of consolidating Britain's hold on her existing Indian and oriental trade routes and keeping foreign influence off them, rather than because of any roseate visions of the future prosperity of the territory claimed [5: *180*]. As a cheap way of asserting paramountcy, the British government agreed to a charter for the British North Borneo Company in 1881, the forerunner of the great African chartered companies. The charter simply gave the company a guarantee of British support and security against the occupation of the territory by a foreign power: it did not allow for commercial monopoly or give the company governmental functions. But it is interesting to note the powerful commercial support behind the company in Britain when it was originally projected [50; 190: chs 1 and 2].

10   Trade, Finance and Informal Empire after 1875

ATTENTION must now be directed to those areas with which Britain retained some kind of informal relationship up to 1914. To what extent did changing economic conditions in Britain and the world lead to changes in these relationships, if at all?

(i) LATIN AMERICA

It was in the period 1860 to 1914 especially that the economic ties between Latin American states and Britain, which had been created over the previous seventy years, began to produce substantial results. Large amounts of British capital flowed in to build railways, harbours, docks and roads which helped to make Latin America into an important supplier of agricultural produce and raw materials. This, in its turn, provided the means to pay interest on the borrowings and to maintain an ever-growing import of manufactured goods from Britain and other advanced industrial countries.

The question as to whether or not this relationship was in any sense an imperialist one is as difficult to answer in this period as it is for the earlier one. Platt, speaking generally, and Ferns, in relation to Argentina, argue strongly that the relationship was roughly an equal one and mutually beneficial [150; 38: 487-91]. Platt has also underlined the extent to which the British maintained their time-honoured policy of non-intervention in local politics except when faced with attacks on lives and property or flagrant breaches of treaty rights and solemn agreements [148: ch. 6]. Britain, for example, resolutely refused to interfere in Argentina when the latter defaulted on loans in 1876 and 1891; in 1891 especially, there was something of a clamour in Britain for a show of strength but the government steadfastly refused to comply [38: 383-6, 465-7]. Neither did the British make any political or economic capital out of the opportunity afforded by the Chilean revolution of 1891: and it has been plausibly argued that the hesitant attempt to influence internal affairs in Mexico during the revolution there was not, as has been alleged, undertaken to bolster the interests of British oil companies but a response to fears for lives and property. When the American government agreed to protect property on her behalf, Britain withdrew [148: *319–20*]. British forbearance in these matters is well illustrated by the case of Venezuela. For over forty years, the bondholders fought an unequal battle against corrupt ministers and officials who appropriated the loans, often refused to pay interest on them, reneged on agreements for orderly repayment and, latterly, committed outrages against British subjects and their property. For most of this period, the British government did little except remonstrate mildly with the Venezuelans despite strong pressure for action from their 'men on the spot'. When the British navy did finally blockade Venezuela it only did so in conjunction with another aggrieved party, the Germans, who precipitated the crisis after 'clearing' their action with the USA. This use of force was principally in aid of British subjects who had suffered personal injury or expropriation; the plight of the bondholders was an important but secondary consideration and the British government refused to act as a debt collector on their behalf. [148: *339–46;* 82]. Also, recent studies of the relations between the Peruvian government and British trading interests there, and between the Argentinian government and the largely British-owned railway companies suggest that in the former case power and influence were equally balanced, while in the latter the initiative lay clearly with local authorities [134; 110].

Nevertheless, there are still many historians who think that the relationship did have an imperialist element, largely on the grounds that British influence and prestige was so great that the British had an over-large say in the running of the economy to the detriment of the long-run development of the Latin American countries. It is argued, for example, that Uruguay, fearful of absorption by her powerful neighbours Argentina and Brazil, relied too heavily on British capital and trade. The local landowning élite benefited from this, but the diversification of the Uruguayan economy was prevented by free trade with unfavourable results for the welfare of the majority of the people [197: *110–14, 116–26*]. Similar arguments about the deleterious consequences of cultural imperialism have been put forward in relation to Brazil [66; 65: esp. ch. 3 and *321–2*] and to Chile. Manteou has recently argued that, in the latter case, the laxity of the landowning élite in allowing nitrate mining to be dominated by British capital prevented the industry from giving Chile the chance to diversify her economy and increase her economic independence. Instead, the most important growth sector in Chile was handed over to a foreign power which enjoyed the cheapest and most agreeable kind of informal control [123].

It should also be noted that there were a few cases when Platt's claims do not seem convincing. The British, for example, leaned rather heavily on the Chileans in the later 1880s to prevent, as they believed, valuable economic concessions being taken out of British hands and offered to American syndicates [133: *88*]. Overall, it is at least arguable that Britain maintained her informal economic empire in Latin America through the agency of the export of capital in vast quantities after 1860.

(ii) FINANCIAL IMPERIALISM IN CHINA

In the late nineteenth century, the British would ideally have liked to maintain their traditional policy in China – support for the maximum degree of freedom of trade which they felt was compatible with the stability of the central government at Peking – but this became steadily more difficult. Reluctantly the British government were forced to abandon their policy of economic *laissez-faire* and became involved in the battle for financial and commercial concessions which accompanied growing power rivalry in China [147; 121: *300–4*].

As early as the 1880s, competition for commercial advantage in China was increasing rapidly. Although the British continued to dominate China's external trade, they were alarmed at the extent to which other governments were prepared openly to back the banks and trading firms of their nationals in the search for exclusive financial and commercial concessions which could eventually become the basis for political power in China. The Foreign Office was reluctant to support British business in the same way, for fear of discriminating unfairly between them. But by 1886, they had come round to the idea, as the Bryce Memorandum makes plain, that if they could use diplomatic pressure to ensure fair treatment for British traders in general, then they would do so. Besides this, it is evident that British officials in China were also allowed to give a good deal of unofficial support to individual firms when they felt it necessary [148: *270–6*; 118].

After 1894, when the Japanese defeat of China made the latter an obvious prey to great power ambition, the British came grudgingly to the conclusion that free trade and the Open Door were redundant policies. When the Chinese were faced with the need to pay an indemnity after the Japanese War, the British government made a valiant attempt to raise an international loan, enlisting the help of Rothschild's and the British-owned Hongkong and Shanghai Bank in the process, for fear that loans might be given by powers with an interest in the partition of China. The first part of the loan went to Russia: but the British were guaranteed a share of the follow-up loans and the

Hongkong and Shanghai Bank was given strong diplomatic support when it sought to raise them [119].

In the late 1890s the pressures on China increased as the great powers began to claim 'spheres of interest'. At first Britain did not find this too objectionable because it seemed to leave open the possibility of free trade in China. It soon became obvious, however, that the other powers, especially Russia and Japan, were intent upon carving out 'spheres of influence' which would give them economic monopolies and lay the groundwork for protectorates in the future [198: chs 3 and 4; 148: 287f.]. Once they realised this, the China traders, who had hitherto supported a vigorous Open Door policy [see p. 61] decided that Britain's interests were best served by claiming exclusive control of the Yangtze Valley, where the bulk of trade was done [144: 217–31]. The British government took up a rather different stance. Besides occupying the port of Wei-hai-wei in 1898, they claimed a 'sphere of interest' in the Yangtze area and took the bulk of the railway concessions available there. They also claimed concessions in other areas as far as possible and, in so doing, they hoped to keep the political power of their rivals out of the Yangtze while at the same time maintaining enough of a foothold in the areas claimed by other powers to prevent these hardening into spheres of influence [198: 91–2]. For example, the British used railway concessions in Manchuria in an attempt to frustrate Russian monopolist ambitions there and to squeeze a favourable trading agreement out of them in 1899 [160].

In the process of gaining and consolidating these concessions, the British moved further and further away from the traditional policy of leaving private enterprise to fend for itself. The Foreign Office was forced into supporting particular banking houses and financial consortia, such as the Hong Kong and Shanghai Bank and the Peking Syndicate, in order to ensure they got concessions. It was also prevailed upon to give public support to some of the undertakings backed by these financial groups to encourage support for them in Britain. No government would go as far as to guarantee the rates of return on any of these projects [148: 294–304]. None the less, the Foreign Office was sometimes willing not only to give diplomatic support to financial syndicates, but also to urge them to take up responsibilities which, on purely economic grounds, the syndicate might have rejected as unprofitable [117].

After 1900, the battle for railway, mining and similar concessions as a means of obtaining influence over the Chinese government became enmeshed in the wider struggles between the great powers which foreshadowed the First World War. One of Britain's great problems in China was that, although she was still the largest trader there and got the greater initial share of the concessions, it was often difficult to persuade investors in Britain to take sufficient interest in them. It was feared that this lack of interest might mean that the control of the concessions would pass into alien hands. Once the entente with France was achieved in 1904, the British, albeit hesitantly, agreed that most of the railway schemes in the Yangste area could best be safeguarded by implementing them jointly with France because the latter could more easily mobilise funds for projects of this kind [34]. Some years later, too, when the USA proposed a much more liberal policy of railway building and operation in northern parts of China than had hitherto existed, the British would have been glad to back them up. They were none the less constrained by the fear that these schemes would prove offensive to Russia and Japan with whom Britain was now allied [33].

Throughout the period, the British government kept to the view that, as the largest trader, she had a vested interest in the unity of China and in the stability of its central government. The policy was powerfully, if unintentionally, aided by Britain's rivals who effectively checkmated each other's political ambitions. When the Manchu dynasty finally collapsed in 1911, Britain played a leading role in organising a consortium of all the major powers which could raise a joint loan to help finance the new government and help it to bring stability as quickly as possible. In the process, the Foreign Office vigorously supported the Hongkong and Shanghai Bank in its attempts to raise Britain's share of the loan. They underwrote this support by dissuading other British financiers from offering competing facilities to China for fear that open competition for finance might provoke political chaos [20].

(iii) THE OTTOMAN EMPIRE

As in China, Britain maintained a predominant position in Turkish trade, but her influence on Turkish politics in the thirty years before the war was threatened by the ability of other European powers to use their diplomatic and financial prowess as a means of gaining a strong position in the Ottoman Empire. And, as in China, the British were forced, albeit reluctantly, to abandon their *laissez-faire* attitudes and join in the fight for concessions [148: *181f.*; 121: *293-7*].

Britain's difficulties in Turkey were rather greater than those in China. Her persistent attempts to persuade the Sultan to liberalise and modernise his regime and her frequent complaints about the brutalities of Turkish policies towards their Christian subjects were greatly resented at the Porte. France and Germany, on the other hand, were more willing to accept the *status quo* in Turkey and to use the influence which this gave them to persuade the Sultan to grant important financial and commercial concessions to their nationals. The British were hampered here, not only by their moral objections to Turkish rule but also by the fact that, whereas the French and German governments could often mobilise capital effectively in the battle for political control, the British government had to rely on the private investor who was largely uninterested in taking up Turkish stock. Despite the fact that Britain was concerned that Turkey, which had strategic significance in relation to her interests in the Mediterranean and the East as well as trading importance, might be partitioned amongst the rival powers, no guarantees on Turkish loans as financial concessions were offered. By the turn of the century, the French were clearly Turkey's senior creditor and German influence was growing rapidly there [148: esp. *187–90*].

Britain's position in Turkey was weakened in 1903 by her failure to gain participation in the grandiose Baghdad railway project inspired by Germany. The Germans did agree to a British share in the project and the government was at first inclined to accept it. The deal, however, fell through when Chamberlain, who was trying hard to increase his influence within the ruling Conservative government, used the undoubted Germanophobic sentiment in Britain at that time as a means of arguing successfully that the participation offered was insultingly small [46: Cf. 32: *180–9*; 21: *48–52*].

In view of their relatively weak position in Turkish finance, the British government showed an interest, after the entente of 1904, in commercial and financial co-operation with the French. Despite French government approval for this, the Ottoman Bank, the French local concern, resisted the idea and little came of the supposed partnership in practice [71]. When the Young Turk revolt proved successful in 1909, amidst British jubilation over its liberal tendencies, the Foreign Office gave discreet support to the formation of the National Bank of Turkey which it hoped would help Britain compete better in the battle for financial control. The Bank was not a success, even though the Foreign Office occasionally discouraged British competitors in order to give it support. It was no more successful than other groups in persuading the investor that Turkish finance was worth the risk. The Foreign Office also showed a disconcerting tendency to drop the Bank if Anglo-French financial co-operation seemed possible; and it was occasionally firmly put in its place when it engaged in deals which the Foreign Office felt were politically objectionable [93].

As the war drew near, Britain's interests in the Middle East came to centre on the Persian Gulf which had great strategic significance in relation to the East – and on the adjacent region of Mesopotamia. Informal control of Muscat, Bahrain and Kuwait was increased between 1880 and 1900 in order to strengthen Britain's position in the Gulf [92: *133–6*]. In 1913/14, agreements were signed with Turkey and with Germany which, *inter alia*, kept the Baghdad railway out of the Gulf region and gave Britain a stake in the railway [32: *225f*.; 21: *168f*.; 148: *215–17*]. In Mesopotamia, strategic reasons for control were reinforced by the discovery of oil. The navy's demand for oil was rising and Mesopotamia seemed the one source of supply which was not within the power of a potential enemy. In pursuit of control, the British government went so far as to buy a controlling share in the Anglo-Persian Oil Company and then encouraged the company to buy out the rival interests competing for the Mesopotamia oil concession in the gift of the Turkish government [88; 94: ch. 4; 148: *239–43*]. The resultant Turkish Petroleum Company, which included some German financial interests, then tendered for the concession which had not actually been granted when war broke out. In the course of the negotiations, the British government often pressurised the financial groups involved into policies they were reluctant to follow; and the National Bank, which was part of a rival syndicate facing the Anglo-Persian Oil Company, was squeezed out of participation despite its association with government interests in the past because the British felt this was diplomatically necessary [94: ch. 5]. The use of local economic interests to further its own wider imperialist designs is also shown in the Foreign Office's vigorous support of the British-owned Smyrna–Aidan railway in its battle for Anatolian railway concessions [120]. Financial and strategic positions of this kind were useful means of upholding political influence and prestige and forestalling partition.

(iv) PERSIA

Throughout the nineteenth century the British interest in Persia revolved around the defence of India. Traditional policy indicated, as in Turkey, that Britain should try to counteract the power of autocratic Russia in the north by encouraging the liberalisation and modernisation of Persia. Unfortunately the private capital which would have been necessary for the success of this grand plan failed to materialise. Added to which, the British were not very anxious to see railways built

65

in Persia, for fear that they might operate to her strategic disadvantage [148: *230–1*].

Russian power steadily increased in Central Asia as a whole and by 1900 Russia was also dominant in Persian trade. Faced with this threat, Britain felt it necessary to take a more deliberate interest in Persian finance. The Imperial Bank of Persia was supported by the Foreign Office and competition with it discouraged: and in 1898 a loan to the Shah was encouraged by Britain which was well aware of the political leverage that Persian indebtedness would bring. After 1900, both the British and Indian governments were involved in loans to the Shah for this purpose [121: *297–300*; 148: *229–30*]. At the same time, the British also gave discreet but effective help to the liberal revolutionaries in Persia between 1905 and 1909 in order to weaken the power of the Shah who was too readily influenced by Russia [102].

By 1907, however, mutual fears of German penetration led both powers to try to settle their differences over Persia. The Russians were agreed to have a 'sphere of interest' in the north, the British in the south and there was a 'neutral' sphere between. Although it was agreed that any party could pursue trade in each other's spheres, the agreement did exclude the possibility of either power gaining important concessions, such as railways, in their respective areas. Other nations were theoretically free to obtain concessions anywhere, but in practice were excluded [102: *736–8*; 148: *233–9*]. These arrangements were often inimical to local British traders and business interests. In fact, Persia provides a classic example of how overall imperial necessities might dictate that local economic and financial interests should be muted or curtailed [148: *244*].

11 Conclusions and Suggestions

THERE is evidently something to be said for Gallagher and Robinson's interpretation of imperial expansion after 1875. Strategic motives – the defence of our existing empire in the East – did have a powerful influence on the decision to expand in East Africa, South Africa and the Middle East; and there is no doubt that many extensions of formal control were undertaken as a last resort when every informal expedient had been exhausted.

It needs to be said immediately, however, that, assuming Gallagher and Robinson are correct about the strategic element in imperial extension in Africa and Asia after 1870, the underlying reason for this was, as they admit, defence of a very precious collection of economic assets in India and her surrounding territories and waterways [157: 9–13; 5: 185–8]. Also – and this is something they do not consider – in so far as extensions of empire were a direct response to increasing great power rivalry, it must be remembered that this widening interest in imperialism was a function of the spread of industrialisation in Europe, especially after 1870. Furthermore, acquisitions for strategic defence purposes might be shaped by different economic forces, ultimately forged in Europe, than those present earlier in the century. Financial organisations like banks or chartered companies had an important role to play in many areas of strategic significance after 1880, such as Persia, East and South Africa and New Borneo [15: 245–6], though it must be emphasised that 'financial imperialism' in the Middle East can be traced back as far as the 1850s.

Besides this, the foregoing review of the evidence suggests more fundamental criticisms of the 'continuity' hypothesis. Gallagher and Robinson do not sufficiently account for the extent to which changes in the metropolitan economy could influence policy overseas. Nor do they consider how far these changes helped to create a vigorous demand for a more positive policy of colonial acquisition or a tightening of informal control; or how they could help to bring about the social and economic collapse which in some areas made formal rule necessary.

Free trade policies survived until the war but came under increasingly severe attack and by 1914 protectionist and preferential policies were competing vigorously for attention. The attack on free trade was one manifestation of the growing anxiety at the relative decline of Britain's industrial strength. Another was a great clamour for the extension of British control to markets in Africa and South-East Asia where businessmen feared French or German occupation might lead to exclusion. Formal annexation in West Africa and perhaps in Burma or Siam was directly influenced by such business pressure. It also had a strong influence in persuading the British government to play a much more active part than hitherto in consolidating informal control in China and Turkey when these empires became the centre of European attention. In the latter case, the British government and its officials took an increasingly direct interest in the promotion of British trade and in wrangling over the loans and concessions which were now an important means of maintaining economic and political power.

Economic changes emanating from Britain and industrial Europe also helped to break down informal collaborative arrangements which the British had relied on in the past. This was the case in West Africa where falling prices for traded commodities after 1870 induced expansions of colonial boundaries and then led to the collapse of indigenous political and economic structures. In Egypt, the steady flow of capital from Europe after 1850 created a weight of indebtedness which brought down the state on which the British had relied for collaborative purposes. The South African crisis, resulting in the Boer War, had its origins in the discoveries of gold which were of first-rate importance to Europe and which also disrupted Britain's informal dominance at the Cape. In both Egypt and South Africa, too, there is some reason for scepticism at Gallagher and Robinson's claim that these areas had only strategic significance to Britain. Recent evidence suggests that the British interest in Egypt was primarily financial. In South Africa, the importance of the defence of the Cape is clear; but it is also true that in the overall result of intervention was a British-dominated capitalist economy which gave not only direct benefit to the metropolis but was also the best defence of the Cape itself.

All in all, there is a great deal to be said for Platt's contention that, in the latter part of the century, British governments took a more active interest in imperial acquisition because of an increasing need for overseas markets, and because of the ramifications of a rapidly expanding export of capital. As for the latter, it is clear that Hobson and his successors did overemphasise the relationship between foreign investment and formal extensions of control. They did not take sufficient account of more purely industrial motives for expansion and they also failed to come to terms with the fact that, especially in areas which had a general strategic significance, it was government which dictated to, and used, the financiers rather than the reverse.* On the other hand, the role of capital export or financial power in helping to maintain or enhance Britain's position in a variety of ways in areas ranging from important markets such as Latin America and the white colonies to small strategic outposts such as New Borneo is obviously of first-rate significance.

Looking at the evidence across the whole period suggests that economic motives were always of importance in prompting Britain to extend her power and influence overseas between 1815 and 1914. It can also be suggested tentatively that the impulse to expand overseas and the form which this expansion took (formal and informal rule) was often determined by changes in the structure and stability of the economy over time, the international ramifications of this and by the changing economic position of Britain relative to her major economic and political rivals. Continuity existed in the sense that economic forces making for imperialism were always present; but these forces were themselves in a constant process of metamorphosis throughout the whole period.

Apart from the obvious need for a closer investigation of links between eighteenth- and nineteenth-century expansion and more study of the effects of British penetration on many of the economies which came under their influence, there is something to be said for trying to look at imperialism from a different angle than that usually assumed in the literature.

Formal or informal imperialism is usually identified with control over either settlement colonies or with 'backward' areas outside Europe. Relationships between the great powers or between the great powers and the smaller nations of Europe are usually treated separately, so that 'imperialism' and 'foreign affairs' are usually seen as distinct categories with little overlap. There may be something to be gained by joining these two streams of inquiry and looking, as Lenin did [109; 180], at imperialism as the struggle for hegemony between the great industrial and military powers, a struggle which involves a whole spectrum of relationships in and out of Europe. A recent study of the relationship between Britain and Portugal, for example, has used the idea of the

---

* For a small but interesting example of the control of financial power by British officials in Malaya see bibliography, no. 176.

'imperialism of free trade' to show that Portugal was as much dominated by Britain as many African or Asian territories [174]. Again, if we are to make full sense of Britain's emergent policy of free trade imperialism in the 1840s it has to be recognised that it was intended principally as a means to eliminate the burgeoning industrial strength of the USA and Western Europe and to help maintain Britain's position as the dominant world power [170: esp. *146–50, 176–81*]. If we look at imperialism in this way, as the economic battle between the great powers, it is possible to argue that the extension of power and influence outside Europe may often play only a minor role in the total process.

To take one last example: one gain from this approach would be to give a different slant to Britain's role in the great-power struggles leading up to the war of 1914. By 1900, Germany was beginning to make a claim for political power and influence throughout the world to match her rise to economic supremacy in Europe. The agreements which Britain made between 1904 and 1907 with France and Russia, her erstwhile enemies, can be seen as part of the coming together of the existing imperial 'have' powers against the menace of German expansion. In 1904, the French accepted Britain's position in Egypt in return for Britain's acquiescence in France's predominance in Morocco [70]: while the Anglo-Russian agreement was largely intended to solve the Persian crisis which had bedevilled relations in the past. The *entente* powers were, in fact, coming together to prevent a redivision of world-wide formal and informal influence by Germany, both in Europe and outside, and were willing to settle some colonial disputes to facilitate this global realignment of interests. Considerations such as those may give a meaning to the great-power alignment before 1914 which is sometimes lacking in purely diplomatic accounts [41; 15: *248–9*]. Further studies of imperialism from this point of view may prove fruitful for the whole of the nineteenth century.

Bibliography

EcHR refers to the *Economic History Review*, second series.

(a) GENERAL BOOKS

There are three general survey books offering different approaches to this question which are well worth reading. They are:

R. Hyam, *Britain's Imperial Century 1815–1914: A Study of Empire and Expansion* (1976).

B. Porter, *The Lion's Share. A Short History of British Imperialism 1850–1970* (1975).

M. Barrett Brown, *After Imperialism*, 2nd ed. (1970).

(b) SPECIALISED ARTICLES AND BOOKS

[1] J. F. A. Ajayi and R. A. Austen, 'Hopkins on Economic Imperialism in West Africa', *EcHR*, xxv (1972). (Cf. 84).

[2] S. Alvinieri, *Karl Marx on Colonialism and Modernisation* (1968).

[3] A. Atmore and S. Marks, 'The Imperial Factor in South Africa in the Nineteenth Century: Towards a Reassessment', *Journal of Imperial and Commonwealth History*, iii 1 (Oct 1974).

[4] M. Barrett Brown, 'A Critique of Marxist Theories of Imperialism', in R. Owen and B. Sutcliffe (eds), *Studies in the Theory of Imperialism* (1972).

[5] J. Bastin, 'Britain as an Imperial Power in South Eastern Asia in the Nineteenth Century', in J. S. Bromley and E. H. Kossman (eds), *Britain and the Netherlands in Europe and Asia* (1968).

[6] W. G. Beasley, *Great Britain and the Opening of Japan 1834–1858* (1951).

[7] G. Blainey, 'Lost Causes of the Jameson Raid', *EcHR*, xviii (1965).

[8] D. C. Blaisdell, *European Financial Control in the Ottoman Empire* (1929).

[9] C. A. Bodelsen, *Studies in Mid-Victorian Imperialism* (1924, repr. 1960).

[10] B. H. Brown, *The Tariff Reform Movement in Great Britain 1881–95* (1943).

[11] I. G. Brown, 'British Financial Advisors in Siam in the Reign of King Chulalongkorn', *Modern Asian Studies*, XII (1978).

[12] L. Brown, *The Board of Trade and the Free Trade Movement, 1830–1842* (1958).

[13] E. Brynn, 'The Emigration Theories of Robert Wilmot Horton', *Canadian Journal of History*, IV (1969).

[14] J. F. Cady, *A History of Modern Burma* (1958).

[15] P. J. Cain, 'European Expansion Overseas 1830–1914', *History*, LIX (1974).

[16] ———— 'Political Economy in Edwardian England. The Tariff Reform Controversy 1903–14', in A. O'Day (ed.), *The Edwardian Age* (1979).

[17] ———— 'Capitalism, War and Internationalism in the Thought of Richard Cobden', *British Journal of International Studies*, 5 (1979), 112–30.

[18] M. E. Chamberlain, 'Clement Hill's Memorandum and British Interests in East Africa', *English Historical Review*, LXXXVII (1972).

[19] ———— 'Sir Charles Dilke and the British Intervention in Egypt, 1882', *British Journal of International Studies*, II (1976).

[20] K. C. Chan, 'British Policy in the Reorganization Loan to China 1912–13', *Modern Asian Studies*, V (1971).

[21] M. K. Chapman, *Great Britain and the Bagdad Railway 1888–1914* (1948).

[22] E. Chew, 'The Reasons for British Intervention in Malaya. Review and Reconsideration', *Journal of the Malayan Branch of the Royal Asiatic Society*, 38 (1965).

[23] J. H. Clapham, 'The Last Years of the Navigation Acts', in E. M. Carus-Wilson (ed.), *Essays in Economic History*, vol. III (1962).

[24] R. O. Collins, 'Origins of the Nile Struggle: Anglo-German Negotiations and the MacKinnon Agreement of 1890', in P. Gifford and W. R. Louis (eds), *Britain and Germany in Africa* (1967).

[25] W. H. B. Court, *British Economic History 1870–1914. Commentary and Documents* (1965).

[26] C. D. Cowan, *Nineteenth-Century Malaya. The Origins of British Political Control* (1961).

[27] G. Daniels, 'The British Role in the Meiji Restoration. A

Reassessment', *Modern Asian Studies*, II (1968).

[28] B. Dean, 'British Informal Empire. The Case of China', *Journal of Commonwealth and Comparative Politics*, XIV (1976).

[29] R. Denoon, '"Capitalist Influence" and the Transvaal Government during the Crown Colony Period, 1900–6', *Historical Journal*, XI (1968).

[30] K. O. Dike, *Trade and Politics in the Niger Delta 1830–1885* (1956).

[31] R. E. Dumett, 'Joseph Chamberlain, Imperial Finance and Railway Policy in British West Africa in the Late Nineteenth Century', *English Historical Review*, XC (1975).

[32] E. M. Earle, *Turkey, The Great Powers and the Bagdad Railway. A Study in Imperialism* (1924).

[33] E. W. Edwards, 'Great Britain and the Manchurian Railways Question 1909–10', *English Historical Review*, LXXXI (1966).

[34] ———— 'The Origins of British Financial Co-operation with France in China 1903–6', *English Historical Review*, LXXXVI (1971).

[35] C. C. Eldridge, *England's Mission: The Imperial Idea in the Age of Gladstone and Disraeli 1868–80* (1973).

[36] S. Fairlie, 'The Nineteenth-Century Corn Law Reconsidered', *EcHR*, XVIII (1965).

[37] H. S. Ferns, 'Britain's Informal Empire in Argentina 1806–1914', *Past and Present*, IV (1953).

[38] ———— *Britain and Argentina in the Nineteenth Century* (1960).

[39] D. K. Fieldhouse, 'Imperialism: An Historiographical Revision', *EcHR*, XIV (1961/2).

[40] ———— *Economics and Empire 1830–1914* (1973).

[41] C. A. Fisher, 'The Changing Dimensions of Europe', *Journal of Contemporary History*, I (1966).

[42] J. E. Flint, *Sir George Goldie and the Making of Nigeria* (1960).

[43] ———— 'Britain and the Partition of West Africa', in J. E. Flint and G. Williams (eds), *Perspectives of Empire* (1973).

[44] F. R. Flournoy, *British Policy Towards Morocco in the Age of Palmerston* (1935).

[45] G. Fox, *Britain and Japan 1858–83* (1969).

[46] R. M. Francis, 'The British Withdrawal from the Bagdad Railway Project in April 1903', *Historical Journal*, XVI (1973).

[47] J. S. Galbraith, 'The "Turbulent Frontier" as a Factor in

British Expansion', *Comparative Studies in Society and History*, II (1960).

[48] ———— 'Myths of the "Little England" Era', *American Historical Review*, CXVII (1961). Reprinted in Shaw (172).

[49] ———— *Reluctant Empire. British Policy on the South African Frontier 1834–54* (1963).

[50] ———— 'The Chartering of the British North Borneo Company', *Journal of British Studies*, IV (1965).

[51] ———— 'The British South Africa Company and the Jameson Raid', *Journal of British Studies*, X (1970).

[52] ———— 'Gordon, MacKinnon and Leopold: The Scramble for Africa 1876–82', *Victorian Studies*, XIV (1970/1).

[53] ———— *MacKinnon and East Africa 1878–95. A Study in the New Imperialism* (1972).

[54] ———— 'Origins of the British South Africa Company', in J. E. Flint and G. Williams (eds), *Perspectives of Empire* (1973).

[55] ———— *Crown and Charter: The Early Years of the British South Africa Company* (1974).

[56] J. Gallagher, 'Foxwell Burton and the New African Policy 1838–42', *Cambridge Historical Journal*, X (1950).

[57] J. Gallagher and R. Robinson, 'The Imperialism of Free Trade, 1815–1914', *EcHR*, IV (1953/4). Reprinted in Shaw (172) and Louis (114).

[58] N. G. Garson, 'British Imperialism and the Coming of the Anglo-Boer War', *South African Journal of Economics*, XXX (1962).

[59] R. J. Gavin, *Aden Under British Rule, 1839–1967* (1975).

[60] R. N. Ghosh, 'The Colonization Controversy: R. Wilmot Horton and the Classical Economists', *Economica*, new ser., XXXI (1964). Reprinted in Shaw (172).

[61] D. R. Gillard, *The Struggle for Asia 1828–1914. A Study in Russian and British Imperialism* (1977).

[62] B. M. Gough, '"Turbulent Frontiers" and British Expansion: Governor James Douglas, the Royal Navy and the British Columbia Gold Rushes', *Pacific Historical Review*, XLI (1972).

[63] C. F. Goodfellow, *Great Britain and South African Confederation 1870–1881.* (1966).

[64] G. S. Graham, *Great Britain and the Indian Ocean. A Study of Maritime Enterprise 1810–50* (1967).

[65] R. Graham, *Britain and the Modernization of Brazil 1850–1914* (1968).

[66] R. Graham, 'Sepoys and Imperialists: Techniques of British Power in Nineteenth-Century Brazil', *Inter-American Economic Affairs*, XXIII (1969).

[67] ————— 'Robinson and Gallagher in Latin America. The Meaning of Informal Imperialism', in Louis (114).

[68] W. D. Grampp, *The Manchester School of Economics* (1960).

[69] M. Greenberg, *British Trade and the Opening of China 1800–42* (1951).

[70] P. Guillen, 'The Entente of 1904 as a Colonial Settlement', in P. Gifford and W. R. Louis (eds), *Britain and France in Africa* (1971).

[71] K. A. Hamilton, 'An Attempt to Form an Anglo-French "Industrial Entente"', *Middle Eastern Studies*, II (1975).

[72] W. K. Hancock, *Survey of British Commonwealth Affairs*, vol. II (1940).

[73] J. D. Hargreaves, *Prelude to the Partition of West Africa* (1963).

[74] ————— 'British and French Imperialism in West Africa 1885–1898', in P. Gifford and W. R. Louis (eds), *Britain and France in Africa* (1971).

[75] ————— *West Africa Partitioned. The Loaded Pause 1885–90* (1974).

[76] P. Harnetty, 'The Indian Cotton Duties Controversy 1894–1896', *English Historical Review*, LXXVII (1962).

[77] ————— 'Lancashire and the Indian Cotton Duties, 1859–62', *EcHR*, XVIII (1965).

[78] ————— *Imperialism and Free Trade. Lancashire and India in the Mid-Nineteenth Century* (1972).

[79] B. Hilton, *Corn, Cash, Commerce. The Economic Policies of the Tory Governments 1815–30* (1977).

[80] J. A. Hobson, 'Capitalism and Imperialism in South Africa', *Contemporary Review*, LXXVII (1900).

[81] ————— *Imperialism. A Study* (1968 ed.).

[82] M. Hood, *Gunboat Diplomacy 1895–1905. Great Power Pressure in Venezuela* (1975).

[83] A. G. Hopkins, 'Economic Imperialism in West Africa. The Case of Lagos 1880–92', *EcHR*, XXI (1968).

[84] ————— 'Economic Imperialism in West Africa: A Rejoinder', *EcHR*, XXV (1972). (Cf. 1.)

[85] ————— *An Economic History of West Africa* (1973).

[86] R. Hyam, 'The Partition of Africa', *Historical Journal*, VII (1964). Reprinted and revised in R. Hyam and G. Martin

(eds), *Reappraisals in Imperial History* (1975).

[87] W. G. Hynes, 'British Mercantile Attitudes towards Imperial Expansion', *Historical Journal*, XIX (1976).

[88] M. Jacks, 'The Purchase of the British Government's Shares in the British Petroleum Company, 1912–14', *Past and Present*, XXXIX (1968).

[89] L. H. Jenks, *The Migration of British Capital to 1875* (1963).

[90] D. J. Jeremy, 'Damning the Flood: British Government Efforts to Check the Outflow of Technicians and Machinery, 1780–1843', *Business History Review*, LI (1977).

[91] H. J. M. Johnstone, *British Emigration Policy 1815–30. 'Shovelling Out Paupers'* (1972).

[92] J. B. Kelly, 'The Legal and Historical Basis of the British Position in the Persian Gulf', *St Antony's Papers*, IV (1958).

[93] M. Kent, 'Agent of Empire? The National Bank of Turkey and British Foreign Policy', *Historical Journal*, XVIII (1975).

[94] ——— *Oil and Empire. British Policy and Mesopotamian Oil 1900–1920* (1976).

[95] V. G. Kiernan, 'Britain's First Contacts with Paraguay', *Atlante*, III (1955).

[96] ——— *Marxism and Imperialism* (1974).

[97] K. K. Kim, 'The Origin of British Administration in Malaya', *Journal of the Malayan Branch of the Royal Asiatic Society*, 39 (1966).

[98] E. R. Kittrell, 'The Development of the Theory of Colonization in English Classical Political Economy', *Southern Economic Journal*, XXI (1964/5). Reprinted in Shaw (172).

[99] I. Klein, 'Salisbury, Rosebery and the Survival of Siam', *Journal of British Studies*, VIII (1968).

[100] ——— 'Britain, Siam and the Malay Peninsula 1906–9', *Historical Journal*, XII (1969).

[101] ——— 'English Free Traders and Indian Tariffs 1874–96', *Modern Asian Studies*, V (1971).

[102] ——— 'British Intervention in the Persian Revolution 1905–1909', *Historical Journal*, XV (1972).

[103] B. A. Knox, 'Reconsidering Mid-Victorian Imperialism', *Journal of Imperial and Commonwealth History*, I (1972/3).

[104] ——— 'Care is More Important Than Haste: Imperial Britain and the Creation of Queensland 1856–9', *Historical Studies. Australia and New Zealand*, LXVI (1976).

[105] R. Koebner and H. D. Schmidt, *Imperialism. The History and*

Significance of a Political Word, 1840–1960 (1964).

[106] O. Köymen, 'The Advent and Consequences of Free Trade in the Ottoman Empire', *Etudes Balkaniques* 2 (1971).

[107] R. V. Kubicek, 'The Randlords in 1895: A Reassessment', *Journal of British Studies*, XI (1972).

[108] D. S. Landes, 'Some Thoughts on the Nature of Economic Imperialism', *Journal of Economic History*, XXI (1961).

[109] V. I. Lenin, 'Imperialism The Highest Stage of Capitalism', *Collected Works*, XXII (1964).

[110] C. Lewis, 'British Railway Companies and the Argentinian Government', in D. C. M. Platt (ed.), *Business Imperialism 1840–1930. An Inquiry Based on British Experience in Latin America* (1977).

[111] T. Lloyd, 'Africa and Hobson's Imperialism', *Past and Present*, LV (1972).

[112] W. R. Louis, 'Sir Percy Anderson's Grand African Strategy', *English Historical Review*, LXXXI (1966).

[113] ———— 'The Berlin Congo Conference', in P. Gifford and W. R. Louis, *Britain and France in Africa* (1971).

[114] ———— (ed.), *Imperialism. The Robinson and Gallagher Controversy* (1975).

[115] O. McDonagh, 'The Anti-Imperialism of Free Trade', *EcHR*, XIV (1962). Reprinted in Shaw (172).

[116] W. D. McIntyre, *The Imperial Frontier in the Tropics 1865–75. A Study of British Colonial Policy in West Africa, Malaya and the South Pacific in the Age of Gladstone and Disraeli* (1967).

[117] D. McLean, 'Chinese Railways and the Towneley Agreement of 1903', *Modern Asian Studies*, VII (1973).

[118] ———— 'Commerce, Finance and British Diplomatic Support in China 1885–6', *EcHR*, XXVI (1973).

[119] ———— 'The Foreign Office and the First Chinese Indemnity Loan 1895', *Historical Journal*, XVI (1973).

[120] ———— 'British Finance and Foreign Policy in Turkey: The Smyrna–Aidan Railway Settlement 1913–14', *Historical Journal*, XIX (1976).

[121] ———— 'Finance and "Informal Empire" before the First World War', *EcHR*, XXIX (1976).

[122] A. K. Manchester, *British Pre-Eminence in Brazil* (1933).

[123] M. Manteou, 'The British in the Atacama Desert: The Cultural Basis of Economic Imperialism', *Journal of Economic History*, XXXVI (1975).

[124] V. Marks, *The First Contest for Singapore 1819–24* (1959).

[125] A. Marsden, *British Diplomacy and Tunis 1875–1902* (1971).

[126] G. Martin, *The Durham Report and British Policy. A Critical Essay* (1972).

[127] ——————— 'Empire Federalism and Imperial Parliamentary Union 1820–70', *Historical Journal*, XVI (1973). Reprinted in R. Hyam and G. Martin (eds), *Reappraisals in Imperial History* (1975).

[128] W. M. Mathew, 'The Imperialism of Free Trade: Peru 1820–70', *EcHR*, XXI (1968).

[129] ——————— 'The First Anglo-Peruvian Debt and Its Settlement 1822–1849', *Journal of Latin American Studies*, II (1970).

[130] ——————— 'Foreign Contractors and the Peruvian Government at the Outset of the Guano Trade', *Hispanic American Historical Review*, LII (1972).

[131] ——————— 'Antony Gibbs and Sons, the Guano Trade and the Peruvian Government 1842–61', in Platt (ed.), *Business Imperialism*. (Cf. 110.)

[132] A. A. Mawby, 'Capital, Government and Politics in the Transvaal 1900–1907. A Revision and a Reversion', *Historical Journal*, XVII (1974).

[133] R. Miller, 'The Making of the Grace Contract: British Bondholders and the Peruvian Government 1885–90', *Journal of Latin American Studies*, VIII (1976).

[134] ——————— 'British Firms and the Peruvian Government 1885–1930', in Platt (ed.), *Business Imperialism* (Cf. 110.)

[135] D. C. Moore, 'Imperialism and "Free Trade" Policy in India 1853–4', *EcHR*, XVII (1964). Reprinted in Shaw (172).

[136] ——————— *Sir Charles Wood's Indian Policy 1853–66* (1966).

[137] W. P. Morrell, *British Colonial Policy in the Mid-Victorian Age* (1969).

[138] D. J. Moss, 'Birmingham and the Campaign Against the Orders in Council and East India Company Charter 1812–13', *Canadian Journal of History*, XI (1976).

[139] A. E. Musson, 'The "Manchester School" and the Exportation of Machinery', *Business History*, XIV (1972).

[140] C. W. Newbury, 'Trade and Authority in West Africa from 1850 to 1880', in L. H. Gann and P. Duignan (eds), *Colonialism in Africa*, vol. I (1969).

[141] R. Owen, 'Egypt and Europe: From French Expedition to

British Occupation', in R. Owen and B. Sutcliffe (eds), *Studies in the Theory of Imperialism* (1972).

[142] ———— 'Robinson and Gallagher on Middle East Nationalism: The Egyptian Argument', in W. R. Louis (114).

[143] H. O. Pappe, 'Wakefield and Marx', *EcHR*, IV (1951/2). Reprinted in Shaw (172).

[144] N. A. Pelcovits, *Old China Hands and the Foreign Office* (1948).

[145] I. R. Phimister, 'Rhodes, Rhodesia and the Rand', *Journal of Southern African Studies*, I (1975).

[146] D. C. M. Platt, 'British Diplomacy in Latin America since the Emancipation', *Inter-American Economic Affairs*, XXI (1967).

[147] ———— 'British Policy During the New Imperialism', *Past and Present*, XXXIX (1968).

[148] ———— *Finance, Trade and Politics in British Foreign Policy 1815–1914* (1968).

[149] ———— 'The Imperialism of Free Trade: Some Reservations', *EcHR*, XXI (1968).

[150] ———— 'Economic Imperialism and the Businessman: Britain and Latin America before 1914', in R. Owen and B. Sutcliffe (eds), *Studies in the Theory of Imperialism* (1972).

[151] ———— *Latin America and British Trade, 1806–1914* (1972).

[152] ———— 'Further Objections to an "Imperialism of Free Trade" 1830–60', *EcHR*, XXVII (1973). Reprinted in Shaw (172).

[153] ———— 'The National Economy and British Imperial Expansion Before 1914', *Journal of Imperial and Commonwealth History*, II (1973/4).

[154] V. J. Puryear, *International Economics and Diplomacy in the Near East. A Study in British Commercial Policy in the Levant 1834–54* (1935).

[155] A. Ramm, 'Britain and France in Egypt 1876–82', in P. Gifford and W. R. Louis, *Britain and France in Africa* (1971).

[156] E. Reynolds, 'Economic Imperialism: The Case of the Gold Coast', *Journal of Economic History*, XXXVI (1975).

[157] R. Robinson and J. Gallagher with A. Denny, *Africa and the Victorians. The Official Mind of Imperialism* (1961).

[158] R. Robinson and J. Gallagher, 'The Partition of Africa', *Cambridge Modern History*, XI (1962). Reprinted in Louis (114).

[159] R. Robinson, 'Non-European Foundations of European Imperialism. Sketch for a Theory of Collaboration', in R.

Owen and B. Sutcliffe (eds), *Studies in the Theory of Imperialism* (1972). Reprinted in Louis (114).

[160] A. L. Rosenbaum, 'The Manchurian Bridgehead. Anglo-Russian Rivalry and the Imperial Railways of North China 1897–1902', *Modern Asian Studies*, x (1976).

[161] G. N. Sanderson, *England, Europe and the Upper Nile 1882–99* (1965).

[162] ———— 'The European Partition of Africa: Coincidence or Conjuncture?', *Journal of Imperial and Commonwealth History*, III (1975).

[163] D. R. Sardesai, *British Trade Expansion in South-East Asia 1830–1914* (1977).

[164] A. Schölch, '"The Man on the Spot" and the English Occupation of Egypt in 1882', *Historical Journal*, XIX (1976).

[165] J. Schumpeter, *Imperialism* (1951).

[166] R. L. Schuyler, *The Fall of the Old Colonial System* (1945).

[167] B. Semmel, *Imperialism and Social Reform 1895–1914* (1960).

[168] ———— 'The Philosophic Radicals and Colonialism', *Journal of Economic History*, XXI (1961). Reprinted in Shaw (172).

[169] ———— 'On the Economics of "Imperialism"', in B. F. Hoselitz (ed.), *Economics and the Idea of Mankind* (1965).

[170] ———— *The Rise of Free Trade Imperialism. Classical Political Economy, the Empire of Free Trade and Imperialism 1750–1850* (1972).

[171] A. G. L. Shaw, 'British Attitudes to the Colonies ca. 1820–50', *Journal of British Studies*, IX (1969).

[172] ———— (ed.), *Great Britain and the Colonies 1815–65* (1970).

[173] G. Shepperson, 'Africa, the Victorians and Imperialism', *Revue Belge de Philologie et d'Histoire*, XL (1962). Reprinted in Louis (114).

[174] S. Sideri, *Trade and Power. Informal Colonialism in Anglo-Portuguese Relations* (1970).

[175] A. W. Silver, *Manchester Men and Indian Cotton 1847–72* (1966).

[176] K. Sinclair, 'Hobson and Lenin in Johore: Colonial Office Policy towards British Concessionaries and Investors', *Modern Asian Studies*, IV (1967).

[177] D. P. Singhal, *The Annexation of Upper Burma* (1960).

[178] Z. Steiner, 'Finance, Trade and Politics in British Foreign Policy 1815–1914', *Historical Journal*, XIII (1970).

[179] J. Stengers, 'L'Imperialisme Colonial de la fin du XIXᵉ siècle', *Journal of African History*, III (1962/3). Translated in P. J. M. MacEwan, *Readings in African History*, vol. II (1968).

[180] E. Stokes, 'Late Nineteenth-Century Colonial Expansion and the Attack on the Theory of Economic Imperialism: A Case of Mistaken Identity?' *Historical Journal*, XII (1969).

[181] ————— 'Imperialism and the Scramble for Africa. The New View', in Louis (114).

[182] ————— 'Uneconomic Imperialism', *Historical Journal*, XVIII (1975).

[183] N. Tarling, 'British Policy in Malay Waters in the Nineteenth Century', in K. G. Tregonning (ed.), *Papers in Malayan History* (1962).

[184] ————— *Imperial Britain in South-East Asia* (1975).

[185] S. Y. Teng, *The Taiping Rebellion and the Western Powers. A Comprehensive Survey* (1971).

[186] E. Thio, 'The British Forward Movement in the Malay Peninsula', in K. G. Tregonning (ed.), *Papers in Malayan History* (1962).

[187] D. Thorner, *Investment in Empire. British Railways and Steam Shipping Enterprise in India* (1950).

[188] B. R. Tomlinson, 'India and the British Empire 1880–1935', *Indian Economic and Social History Review*, XII (1975).

[189] L. Trainor, 'The British Government and Imperial Economic Unity 1890–5', *Historical Journal*, XIII (1970).

[190] C. K. Tregonning, *Under Chartered Company Rule. North Borneo 1881–1946* (1958).

[191] C. M. Turnbull, 'The Origin of British Control in the Malay States Before Colonial Rule', in J. Bastin and R. Roolvnick, *Malayan and Indonesian Studies* (1964).

[192] J. E. Tyler, *The Struggle for Imperial Unity 1868–95* (1938).

[193] J. M. Ward, *British Policy in the South Pacific (1786–1893)* (1948).

[194] ————— *Empire in the Antipodes. The British in Australasia 1840–60* (1966).

[195] J. B. Williams, *British Commercial Policy and Trade Expansion 1750–1850* (1972).

[196] D. N. Winch, 'Classical Economics and the Case for Colonization', *Economica*, new series, XXX (1963). Reprinted in Shaw (172).

[197] D. Winn, 'British Informal Empire in Uruguay in the

Nineteenth Century', *Past and Present*, LXXIII (1976).

[198] L. K. Young, *British Policy in China 1895–1902* (1972).

[199] S. H. Zebel, 'Fair Trade: An English Reaction to the Breakdown of the Cobden Treaty System', *Journal of Modern History*, XII (1940).

[200] ———— 'Joseph Chamberlain and the Genesis of Tariff Reform', *Journal of British Studies*, VII (1967).

Index